POWER TO THE PUBLIC

POWER
TO THE
PUBLIC

The Promise of
Public Interest Technology

TARA DAWSON McGUINNESS
AND HANA SCHANK

PRINCETON UNIVERSITY PRESS
PRINCETON & OXFORD

Published by Princeton University Press
41 William Street, Princeton, New Jersey 08540
6 Oxford Street, Woodstock, Oxfordshire OX20 1TR

press.princeton.edu

All Rights Reserved
LCCN 2020950666
ISBN 9780691207759
ISBN (e-book) 9780691216638

British Library Cataloging-in-Publication Data is available

Editorial: Peter Dougherty, Alena Chekanov
Production Editorial: Elizabeth Byrd
Production: Erin Suydam
Publicity: James Schneider, Kate Farquhar-Thomson

Jacket art and design by Derek Thornton / Notch Design

This book has been composed in Arno with Futura for display

Printed on acid-free paper. ∞

Printed in the United States of America

10 9 8 7 6 5 4 3 2 1

T.M.
for my parents Mary & Terry McGuinness, who taught
me everything I know about love, kindness, and
helping others

H.S.
For my mother, Diane Schank, who moved to help care
for my kids so I could work in public interest technology

&
for future public interest technologists,
who will change the world

CONTENTS

PREFACE

Public Interest Technology and Why It Matters

THE WORLD IS ON FIRE. We hope by the time you read this book that is not so, or less so. But the tail of a global pandemic and the ensuing economic crisis is likely to be long—years, perhaps decades, of remaking ourselves, our systems, and our institutions. Now more than ever we need a new generation of public problem solving that ends what ails us. The world needs governments and nonprofits that provide meaningful help and change.

A new practice is emerging around the globe and making a difference—one that better positions organizations to be responsive problem solvers. This practice is grounded in three essential elements: **design** informed by real human needs, the use of real-time **data** to guide problem solving, and a focus on **delivery** in order to continuously learn and improve.

These elements are not new on their own. What is new is that across the world, people are using this combination of approaches to serve people better and solve problems at their root. This signals the creation of a new field, which has been termed public interest technology by those working in and researching the space.[1] We define public interest technology as the application of design, data, and delivery to advance the public interest and promote the public good in the digital age.

The field builds on other traditions from existing fields, which we will explore. What makes public interest technology different is that it has the potential to operate on a very large scale and is accompanied by a mindset about the role that government should play in people's lives: government must help, *really* help. It should not present barriers, complications, or confrontations. **There is no solving the world's hardest problems without governments and institutions that really work for people.** Public interest technology provides a strategy to do just this.

Design

One of the challenges today's problem solvers face, as a result of our world's increased complexity, is the distance between deciders, lawmakers, public officials, and those whom they serve. When President Lincoln presided over a country of thirty-one million residents, he was perhaps the first U.S. president to conduct user research. He would open the doors to the White House after breakfast to hear from not only government officials, but citizens. Noah Brooks, a journalist and a friend of Lincoln, wrote of these listening sessions: "With admirable patience and kindness, Lincoln hears his applicant's requests, and at once says what he will do, though he usually asks several questions, generally losing more time than most businessmen will by trying to completely understand each case."[2]

But as the U.S. population has grown tenfold since Lincoln's time, the distance between government leaders and those they serve has grown far more. While the new millennium brought a ruthless focus on delivering for customers in the private sector—testing messages and imagery and even tweaking the timing of e-mails to increase customer response—this modern tool kit did not permeate government. For government to function well in the modern era, this must change. Close proximity, understanding, research, and constant program testing with the people you are trying to serve is essential to getting public policy and public programs right in the digital age.

To improve how government works today we need to build a tighter feedback loop between the people and those who design policies for them. From a book ordered on Amazon to a Lyft ride, today's companies are constantly learning, testing, and seeking data and feedback. There is no reason we can't bring these tools to bear on solving the world's hardest problems, from reminding new parents to show up for doctor visits through text messages to reaching taxpayers in need with automated emergency stimulus payments. Deep user research and behavioral nudges keep us glued to our phones and earn billions for the private sector. Why shouldn't these tools be applied to improve our quality of life, to keep us healthy and safe, and to reach the most vulnerable with needed, essential services?

Data

Many modern companies use data to stay connected to their customers, learn from their habits, and improve sales. These companies are constantly tracking, gathering, analyzing, and testing what works and using this data to make decisions—even for processes as simple as selling a cup of coffee. Starbucks uses data to determine everything from where to open a store to what to put on a menu.[3] Starbucks menus are digital, allowing the company to learn what is working and what is not, and to optimize the menu without repainting a sign. What you see on a Starbucks menu may differ throughout the day or in a particular season or location.

Conversely, Jennifer Pahlka, founder and former executive director of Code for America, a nonprofit focused on bringing the effective use of technology and design to the public sector, describes the public sector's use of data as being "like asking a pilot to fly a transcontinental flight with only after-the-fact, unreliable estimates of her airspeed, heading, and altitude."[4]

Using, collecting, and analyzing data to better see those you are serving is imperative for the public sector. If Starbucks can use data to better understand when their customers want a Frappuccino, think of the endless possibilities for governments and nonprofits to use these same tools to help the people they serve.

Delivery

The final aspect of public interest technology is the capacity to rapidly test, learn, and then improve via a minimum viable product (MVP). In practice, this means running a small pilot test of how something might work, and making improvements quickly before broadening usage. Though a focus on MVPs and a culture of rapid learning have guided the rise of many modern companies, these methods are not new. In the 1940s, W. Edwards Deming evangelized a "plan, do, study, act" learning cycle for the private sector.[5] This approach has more recently been applied in hospitals and clinics through the work of improvement science, where testing and improving one area of care can bring about changes in outcomes.[6] Some teams in the public sector are able to think in an MVP framework. Most do not.

———

Preparing organizations to thrive in the world today isn't a one-and-done operation like upgrading to a new computer. It is a process. It takes work. New tools are important, but these tools cannot be digitized versions of overly complex paper systems.

New tools don't work without understanding the humans who use them, their skills, their work, and their challenges. And new tools won't fix a broken policy or a convoluted process, just as overlaying a microprocessor on top of a Rube Goldberg device won't make the device more efficient. The Rube Goldberg device needs to be streamlined and designed with users first, before it can be sped up and digitized.

In the UK, Canada, India, Estonia, and Australia, digital transformation is already under way at a nation-state level. In this book we will make these practices visible and show that they are already transforming lives for the better across the globe. While we focus on U.S. cases, which we know best, the United States is by no means the only leader in delivery practices—this work is truly global, and the UK and others have led in federalizing these practices first.

Make no mistake, the practice of public interest technology is not a panacea. Quite often data, user feedback, and piloting will set free a Pandora's box of new challenges. These challenges come with the territory—once you start digging into problems in a meaningful way, you often find another layer of problems. And problem solving in the digital age, by definition, often involves applying new technologies that have the potential to cause harm or be misused. Despite the challenges and imperfections, a fresh approach that puts people at the center is essential to reconcile today's public problems.

Our Principles

Embedded in this book is a core set of principles:

First, *there is no solving the world's hardest problems without government.* While universities, hospitals, nonprofits, and companies have important roles, there is none like the role of government.

The private sector, too, is limited in the role it can play. Often, when government fails or becomes too complex, a private company springs up to take advantage of the opportunity. This is evident in industries like immigration paperwork filers, global entry application apps, and tax assistance firms. But while these industries exist to help people interact with government, they cannot take the place of processing immigrants, expediting entry into the country, or collecting taxes.

Second, although we write about where governments have failed, *we believe deeply in government and the people who work in government at all levels.* Government workers are not the problem. Government is not the problem. The problems lie in the systems, incentives, and structures government inhabits, which are no longer aligned well with serving its citizenry in a digital era.

Third, technology can play a critical role, but it is never the solution alone. Data science, sensors, algorithms, and artificial intelligence on their own will not bring about transformation. Change lies in technology designed explicitly to solve clearly defined problems. Technology does not work in a vacuum. Additionally, technology by its very nature is ever-changing. At one time the combustion engine was the very cutting edge of technology. What is new today will be outdated tomorrow. Those who pin progress to a single technology or to a narrow definition of what technology is do so at their own peril.

Finally, the role of government should be to help all people. Period. Government should not be designed to keep people out, or be a burden to the very people it is meant to serve. Government exists to do the things we cannot do alone, to help us in our hour of need, and to allow humanity to flourish.

How to Use This Book

The first half of this book, chapters 1 through 4, tells the story of a loose network of problem solvers who are using public interest technology to solve public problems in novel, effective, and impressive ways. We begin by painting a picture of the current state of problem solving, and why public interest technology is so very needed. Next, we break down the elements that make up the practice of public interest technology, giving real-world examples of how people are using each of the three tools to work on challenges like homelessness, foster care, and suicide prevention.

The second half of the book outlines the evolving structure of public interest technology and points to the way in which all levels of government—city, state, and local—and nonprofits can help to operationalize the practice.

Who Should Read This Book

This book is for people who are—or will be—in a position to take on public problems. Whether you are the head of a government agency, a start-up entrepreneur seeking to innovate a solution, a program manager at a nonprofit, or a policy student, our aim in writing this book is to equip you with an understanding of the elements of problem solving in the digital age. This book is an introduction to the field and practice of public interest technology, but it is not a how-to manual. Our goal is to leave you with an understanding of what public interest technology is, and why it is now an indispensable piece of any public problem solver's tool kit. For those ready to take action, we have provided a list of resources at the end to help you find your way to others in the field.

Who We Are

There is something about the speed with which technology changes and the opacity of the field that encourages people to position themselves as tech experts when they in fact have little hands-on experience. As we write this book, there are lots of people saying words like "design thinking" or "machine learning" or "artificial intelligence" who may not fully understand the history or practice of those terms. This technical pretending is so common when it comes to using agile (if you don't know what that is, don't worry—we will get into it later) that people use a handy acronym to refer to the practice: AINO (Agile in Name Only). For this reason, we think it is important to state up front both our technical and nontechnical bona fides. Public interest technology is a practice we are both deeply engaged in and have been for several years, and builds logically on our very different but overlapping backgrounds.

One of us is a technologist turned public servant. The other is a public servant turned tech translator. Though we wrote this book from two very different perspectives, we believe strongly that problem solving in the digital age requires both viewpoints—more technologists at the public problem-solving table (like Hana) and more public leaders who are tech-fluent enough to expand the classic toolbox (like Tara).

Hana grew up with a computer in her house, which is only noteworthy because she grew up in the 1970s. As the child of one of the pioneers of artificial intelligence, Hana learned to code shortly after learning to write. She spent the early part of her career at one of the Big Five consultancies, working adjacent to some of the humongous transformation projects of the mid-1990s, developing training materials, advising on interface design, and once writing a piece of the login code. Many of the giant systems her consultancy built back then are the very same ones causing so many problems today. Once the Internet happened, Hana left big consulting to work on launching many of the first websites for Fortune 500 companies and start-ups. Over the past two decades she has been an information architect, user experience designer, and user researcher for countless sites, apps, and tools. In 2016 she joined the United States Digital Service (USDS), where she ran the relaunch of the Global Entry website and conducted research into ELIS (the immigration system we discuss in chapter 1), among other projects. Today Hana works exclusively in the public sector, running public interest technology projects and research.

Tara has spent her career in public service, working for nonprofits, congressional offices, and think tanks, and in the federal government, including the White House. She has worked as an organizer, a Hill staffer, a strategist, and a policy advisor on issues including climate change, healthcare, and equity. She was responsible for leading the effort to sign up millions of Americans for free and low-cost health insurance through Obamacare. It was this deep engagement on the team implementing the Affordable Care Act—in both its failures and its turnaround—that sparked her obsession with delivery and how policy reaches those who need it most. For several years, she has been researching and writing and teaching (graduate policy students) about the importance of data, design, and delivery to the success or failure of public policy. Today she runs a lab dedicated to bringing these delivery practices to bear on family economic security.

While there is no perfect recipe for improving people's lives, there are some key ingredients without which no formula will succeed. This book will lay out those essential ingredients. We will show you how public interest technology pioneers are tackling the world's hardest problems and succeeding. We will introduce you to people who are experimenting with visionary approaches and to organizations that are undertaking their work differently and helping people thrive. Through the chapters that follow you will meet leaders who are grounding their work in the needs and lived experiences of those they serve. You will understand why data is an essential part of helping governments save lives across the globe. And we will share stories of how nonprofits and governments solve problems through rapid experimentation, saving time and more effectively meeting the needs of the people they serve.

If we have done our job well, this book will be both a source of inspiration and a map to help you start to chart your own course. Our goal in writing this book is to show you what it looks like when public problem solving really works, and the steps you can take to get there. We have provided you with a compass. It is up to you to make the voyage.

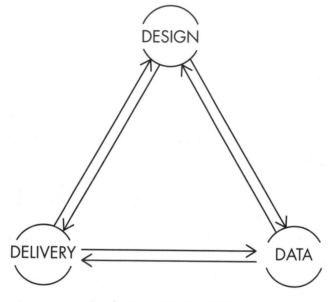

People-Centered Problem Solving

1

The Current State of
Problem Solving

IN 2005, THE UNITED STATES Citizenship and Immigration Services (USCIS), the successor to the Immigration and Naturalization Service (INS) and the federal agency responsible for green cards and citizenship applications, began a project to digitize the nation's immigration system.[1]

At that time anyone who wanted to stay in the country for a long period of time, or those who wanted to become American citizens, would fill out a paper form and mail it to USCIS. Those applications would then be packed into boxes, put into the back of a truck, and driven around the country for processing. All forms requiring an interview made their way through the National Processing Center in Kansas City, and then back out to regional processing centers. As they were driven around the country, at each stop the applications grew into hundred- and sometimes thousand-page files, as immigration officers and others added evidence and interview reports and other documentation. There were several computer systems that handled individual tasks such as scheduling interviews with applicants, but for the most part the process of doing anything with USCIS—replacing a lost green card, renewing an expired card, or applying to become a citizen—occurred entirely on paper. USCIS had decided it was time to move over to digital, partially to keep pace with the rest of the world but primarily to speed up the processing time, increase security, and better serve applicants. For context, that same year, Apple rolled out three new iPods, the cities of San Francisco and Philadelphia began offering free citywide WiFi, and Google launched its geographic app, Google Earth.[2]

Eleven years and $1 billion later, USCIS had managed to digitize two out of ninety-four different types of immigration forms into a system called ELIS (Electronic Immigration System), named in a nod to Ellis Island. The first design of the system—ELIS 1—had begun during the George W. Bush administration, and seven years into development was such a dysfunctional mess that USCIS was forced to scrap it and start again.

The development of gargantuan technical systems often takes much longer than anyone expects and involves multiple types of failure. In 2011, the UK was forced to kill a £4.6 billion system that had been in development for nine years, meant to streamline the National Health System's record keeping.[3] In 2019, after nine years of work and at a cost of $2.2 billion, the Canadian federal payroll system's migration to a new platform failed so spectacularly that thousands of Canadians went without pay for weeks.[4]

In government, technical failure often doesn't result in prohibiting the companies responsible from bidding on or landing future contracts. After the failed rollout of a system for public assistance built by Deloitte, the state of Rhode Island renewed the company's contract.[5] Of course, big tech failures happen in the private sector too—Boeing's disastrous development of the 737 Max is a recent, deadly example. But perhaps most crucially, unlike in the public sector, these failures typically don't put people's lives at risk (which is what drew so much attention to the Boeing failure). If Instagram goes down for a week, the rent still gets paid (unless you are an influencer who relies on Instagram for your livelihood), dinner still makes its way to the table, food and prescription drugs are still safe to consume, streets continue to be repaired, electricity still reaches your house, and so on.

The challenges ELIS faced only came to President Barack Obama's attention when the lack of a functional system threatened to interfere with the implementation of his executive actions on immigration. The new policies, which included Deferred Action for Parents of Americans (DAPA)—a policy that would have granted work permits and protection from deportation for illegal immigrants whose children were U.S. citizens or green card holders—meant that USCIS would be processing an additional four million people in a system that at capacity could likely process only seven million a year.[6] Obviously that was not going to work.

President Obama had already seen what happened when a policy his administration was intent on implementing ran afoul of technology with the launch of the Affordable Care Act (aka Obamacare). That launch had been devastating for government workers and citizens alike, as the site crashed under the user load, and failed time and again as users tried to shop for health insurance plans. Obama was not going to take the same risk this time around, so to ensure that ELIS would be able to handle the additional load, he dispatched a small technical team to take a look at what would need to happen at USCIS as they prepared to launch DAPA. (Welcome to a book full of stories about government, where there will be overabundant use of acronyms.)

Enter an Engineer

When software engineer Brian Lefler arrived at the bland USCIS office building a few blocks from Washington, D.C.'s Union Station, his expectation was that he would be writing code. He'd taken a leave of absence from his job at Google after hearing a pitch on how he could use his skills to help his country by Mikey Dickerson, who had been involved in the Healthcare.gov rescue and was in the process of recruiting people for the United States Digital Service (USDS). That sounded like an interesting opportunity, so he joined USDS, a cadre of experienced designers, engineers, researchers, and product managers embedded throughout the federal government. But after just a few days at USCIS, he discovered that a lack of quality code was not ELIS's problem.

The office was filled with software engineers who were more than capable of doing technical work. But the engineers were staffed through contracting agencies, so they were not USCIS employees and therefore didn't have anyone on the government side who could push them on the technical details. The federal career staff at USCIS were used to overseeing a paper-based process, but most were not experienced technologists. Although they were intimately familiar with the business processes and the legal and policy requirements, they lacked the skills and knowledge required to directly manage the development of a complex technical system. Without seasoned technologists on the federal team, questions about how to allocate engineers to tasks, prioritization of those tasks, and how system features should be implemented were inexpertly answered. Contracted engineers who needed these questions answered to move forward found themselves stuck.

Also missing was an incentive structure for contractors that led to speedy, solid development practices. Instead, contractors were beholden to corporate practices that had evolved over years of government bringing in contractors to build systems instead of investing in the capacity to do this in-house. As a result, the vast majority of government projects that require technical expertise are handled by private companies. And many companies, eager to lock these lucrative contracts in place for as long as possible, try to build in naturally recurring needs for their skills.[7] Because there was no one on the USCIS side who could push back on ELIS from a technical perspective in the project's early days, the contractor—IBM—had seized an undue amount of control over the design of the system. The contractor had designed ELIS so that it relied heavily on IBM products, even when those products did not benefit the processing speed or help people to use the system.[8]

"ELIS 1 was built to generate software licenses and sustain them in perpetuity, first and foremost. Then secondly to serve the agency's needs," observed Lefler. "It didn't work. ELIS 1 was unquestionably worse than paper, and it was ultimately turned down."[9] When ELIS 1 was released, USCIS discovered that it slowed down the processing of immigration forms by a multiple of five.[10] You read that correctly. The digital system took five times as long as paper to move applicants through.

When Lefler and a handful of others recruited by Dickerson's pitch sat down at USCIS, ELIS 1 had already been scrapped, and work on ELIS 2 had begun. This was in large part thanks to the arrival of Mark Schwartz, who had been hired in 2012 into the chief information officer (CIO) role at USCIS from the private sector.

"I was looking around for what might be the next thing. At some point I was reading an article about how screwed up government IT was, and being the arrogant person that I am I thought, *Well, I'll just go fix it,*" Schwartz remembers.[11]

Schwartz recognized the problem with IBM's efforts to build ELIS as "what usually happens with a monolithic waterfall project" and worked to extricate USCIS from the contract. "Waterfall" is an older methodology for building technology products, in which teams might spend years building a massive system and then release the whole thing with the flick of a switch, or what is referred to as "big bang." Schwartz was experienced with a methodology known as "agile," which has largely replaced waterfall as the go-to process for building technology. Agile allows teams to rapidly research, build, and test small portions of a system, adding on as they go, so that products can be released and improved upon quickly, rather than engineers spending years building one ginormous system. In line with modern thinking, Schwartz had begun to shift USCIS into an agile process. But moving an organization into a methodology that was largely new to them, on a project that they had been engaged in for years, was a bit like trying to turn a battleship loaded with elephants.

A lack of support from qualified staff made it especially difficult to change much of anything, says Eric Hysen, a product manager on the USDS team. "There was finally a realization that the old way wasn't working, and there were some champions, but they didn't have anyone to support them," he explains. "You had Mark [Schwartz] shouting words like *agile* and *cloud* and *dev ops*, and his staff were struggling to figure out what those meant and trying to adapt contracts accordingly."[12] It's not that USCIS staff didn't want to support the project, but they didn't know how. They were missing the context and skills needed to undertake a successful project using a methodology that was foreign to them.

Not only were the USCIS staff and contractors scrambling to adjust to a new way of doing work, but the federal government itself continued to evaluate the project's progress as though it were using a traditional approach rather than trying something new. The evaluations didn't go very well. The reports from the Office of the Inspector General (an independent oversight body housed in each federal agency that ensures that agency work is efficient, effective, and lawful) on ELIS grew increasingly alarmist and combative as time passed and no massive system was launched. The reports dismissed the switch to agile, and continued to question why the entire system wasn't being built in one mammoth effort.[13]

"It was like peeling back the layers of a hundred-layer onion, where every time there's something that cements doing things in a way that was so out of date I'd heard about it in college, learning about the old days of computing," Hysen said. "These were not even things that I did earlier in my career."[14]

The shift from waterfall to agile was as monumental and confusing as if the office had been using pneumatic tubes to send communications, and someone had walked into the building with e-mail.

Digital Is Not Always Better

Part of ELIS's problem was that the development timeline had stretched so long that the way technology was built shifted over the course of the project. In 2005, while a waterfall approach might have been considered slightly outdated, it wouldn't have been ludicrous to employ. But by 2014, when Lefler, Hysen, and others joined the team, waterfall was a pneumatic tube. Even more problematic: while ELIS 1 was in large part doomed by the fact that there was no one on staff to help move the team over to agile, ELIS 2 faced an even bigger problem in the agency's assumption that digital would unquestionably be better than paper.

This was taken as an article of faith, and it turned out to be disastrously wrong.

In some cases, based purely on the task someone was looking to complete, paper was superior to digital. Lefler sounded a bit awestruck as he recounted watching immigration officers work their way through immense case files, searching specifically for aliases that an applicant might have used. Some applicants use multiple names for cultural reasons, so this is an issue that comes up quite a bit, but immigration officers have developed a simple system for resolving it. As Lefler explains:

> They will put a little thing on their thumbs so that they can rifle through a giant pack of documents very quickly. The operator has memorized anything that is a government-looking document, that might have a name on it. As they see a document at a glance that's probably going to have a name on it, they'll check the name and then they'll continue rifling through it. They go through giant stacks of paper extremely fast. There was no way to implement that electronically, short of five years of machine learning and OCR [optical character recognition] technology. It cannot be done.[15]

A common mistake people make when trying to improve or modernize something is believing that digital will always be better. But digitizing a broken paper process doesn't make it better. Sometimes it makes it worse. In the case of ELIS, the team looked at their job as one where they took what was on a form, digitized it, and called it done. They did not factor in the colossal amount of filing, categorizing, and handwritten note making that the people processing forms did on a daily basis. They didn't think about how digitization would impact the people who used the forms and how they used them. USCIS employees worked with these forms every day. They marked them up with notes and flagged ones that needed additional work, or put sticky notes on forms that required interviews, or placed the ones that needed a supervisor to take a look on a special shelf in the office. In digitizing only the forms, ELIS accounted for a small percentage of the work required to move immigration forms from start to finish. Without the remaining pieces, the forms simply couldn't move.

"Digital was not better than paper because the system assumed a process that was different from how adjudicators actually did the work," explains Vivian Graubard, a founding member of USDS. "These files were huge but also they often had to flip back and forth between pages. So it was faster for adjudicators to print out the entire application and review that way than to review on screen."[16]

Dana Chisnell, a user experience designer and researcher who was also part of the USDS team, describes what she found when she arrived onsite. "They'd paid no attention whatsoever to the usability of the system, and there was no vocabulary to paying attention to the needs of users."[17]

In other words, in designing the system no one had thought that interviewing the front line government workers who would be using the system was important to determining how ELIS should function. The ELIS team had thoroughly documented business processes and data flows, but none of the developers really understood how immigration officers did their jobs. The team did have subject matter experts (SMEs) advising them, but in many cases these SMEs hadn't been in the field in a long time.[18] They also rotated out every few months, so people got different information based on which SME they worked with. Along with Mollie Ruskin, another USDS designer on the project, Chisnell took a trip to a service center in Nebraska to get a better handle on what people in the field did with the paper forms. The people in the service center seemed thrilled to see Chisnell and Ruskin. No one from headquarters had ever asked how they did their work.

But after the designers returned from their trip out to the service center full of new information, HQ saw the value of visiting service centers and began regularly sending teams. Chisnell also suggested to the leadership on ELIS that it would be helpful for programmers on the project to see firsthand how immigration officers worked. The first group came back excited to implement their new findings. Once they got to work, they were able to build functionality faster and more accurately, now that they had a better understanding of what people out in the field needed to do in their jobs. The team ended up creating a schedule to get everyone out for a field visit.

But even with all the improvements made by both the USCIS team and USDS, ELIS 2 dragged along in a semi-usable state for years. By 2016, after the system had been rolled out for additional forms, immigration officers were using ELIS grudgingly and with a fair amount of seething hatred. One field office made a video of themselves kicking a computer with "ELIS" taped to it on paper.[19]

In addition to the bad feelings, immigration officers had developed a series of work-arounds to make ELIS usable. Their offices were often filled with stacks of files in varying locations to make up for the lack of a filing system in ELIS. The system was slow and prone to outages. For a period of time in 2016 one of the most-used forms was taken offline while a team worked on stabilizing it. Basements staffed with contractors tasked with clicking a single button or unsticking cases that were caught up accidentally due to a faulty ELIS algorithm were filled to overflowing in Arlington, Virginia, costing USCIS uncounted stacks of dollars a day.

One employee at a processing center noted that a large portion of her day was occupied by undoing what ELIS had automated for her. "I spend three and a half hours every morning un-assigning the cases that don't have evidence and going through the ones that do," she told researchers in September 2016.[20]

Unclear Goals

In attempting to digitize the immigration process, USCIS had taken on a massively complex analog system. Immigration officers dealt with about a hundred different forms, each requiring its own process. Those forms were shipped across the country from storage spaces to field offices and service centers in order to serve millions of applicants every year. Adding to the complexity, Mark Schwartz says, USCIS wasn't entirely sure *why* they were going digital, beyond the vague notion that things would be better on a computer. Without hard metrics guiding their goals, the ELIS team never knew whether they'd been successful.

"They had the idea that they needed to get off paper, but they had all sorts of expectations about why—what they would accomplish by getting off of paper—and it wasn't clear what the priorities were or how they were going to actually link getting off of paper to accomplishing those particular benefits," Schwartz says.[21]

The director of USCIS, Léon Rodriguez, struggled to keep abreast of the massive technology project running off the rails that had been deposited at his feet after his confirmation hearing in 2014. Rodriguez had worked in government for decades, but he'd never before encountered a technology project that was "going off a cliff," commenting that "the level of problems that we kept having with ELIS was unprecedented in the face of all my prior experiences. Even in county government I had never seen the kinds of repeated problems, almost to the day that I walked out the door, that we had with ELIS."[22]

Rodriguez was an expert in policy and law, but technology had not been a big part of his management concerns in prior posts. ELIS was the first time he'd heard the term "agile." Reflecting on what could have been done to help get his arms around the responsibility of righting a technology project gone wrong, Rodriguez says he wishes he could have had something like a technology translator to lay out significant issues in nontechnical terms—a dedicated senior person to be his ELIS liaison, in the way government officials often have policy liaisons. But there was no one at USCIS to play that role, and because it is only relatively recently that technology has become the common medium for policy delivery, it isn't a role that normally exists.

According to Rodriguez, "You [need to] have somebody at a very senior management level who understands what's going on with the technology development and can translate it for you. In retrospect, I would have wanted to have somebody around who was consistently available, watching what was going on with those issues."[23]

The gap that Rodriguez identifies is one that many public sector organizations struggle with as technology plays an ever-increasing role in how the world conducts business—how to oversee a technology project if you have never done so before and lack technical knowledge. Rodriguez's suggestion that agencies establish a technology translator–type role would certainly solve this problem, and it is an idea we have brought before Congress.[24] In practice, this would be an executive-level role whose sole purpose is to keep tabs on any large, mission-critical technical projects within an agency. This means that any agency running a vital project that involves a technical build should ensure that there is someone on staff with a technical background—this doesn't need to be someone who can write code, but a person who has experience launching products and systems—who can think strategically about technology as it relates to policy and problem solving.

Relying on Old Processes in a Rapidly Changing World

We are not sharing the story of ELIS because it is unique. It's not that the staff heading USCIS were inept. The employees and contractors were good at what they did. And the process ELIS was trying to digitize was byzantine, but not unduly so. Many a government agency or big organization has been shaken by attempts to keep up with the times by launching a tech project, only to have the project lead them to the pit of despair. We chose to begin with the story of ELIS because it illustrates the varied reasons big government IT projects fail. Technology is viewed as a way to fix a policy or process that is broken. An agency fails to understand the underlying issues slowing down a process, or even what the agency's core goals are in building a new system. Staff and leadership often lack the technical know-how required to make decisions about modern projects. And so many more.

One of the challenges facing governments—one that ELIS ran headlong into and hit like a cement wall—is that government processes are old. Companies in the private sector evolve or die. Government and other civil society institutions, from the Red Cross to the United Way, don't have that option. They have to work—lives depend on them. The system ELIS attempted to digitize was built for a different time, when work involved paper and mail and stamps. In 2018, USCIS processed over 750,000 applications from immigrants seeking to become U.S. citizens—only one of the many processes ELIS attempted to digitize.[25] Comparatively, between 1892 and 1954, Ellis Island—the first federal immigration processing center in the nation—processed an average of 10,000 people a day, a number that included *all* foreign arrivals into New York, not only those seeking citizenship.[26]

These changes are not limited to immigration. Nearly every dimension of life has seen dramatic transformation over the past fifty years. The complexity, scale, and speed of everything from profit-making to computer processing have increased.

In the past decade, smartphones have turned millions of individuals into publishers of their own videos, audios, and texts. No longer do governments, powerful media companies, and private presses have exclusive rights to edit and control information. There used to be a printing press in every town. Today anyone with a cell phone can be a publisher. In *The Zero Marginal Cost Society*, Jeremy Rifkin estimated that today nearly a third of Earth's inhabitants are publishers.[27]

Schools and academies were once restricted to physical buildings populated by the teachers who were available in any given town or city. Today, hundreds of millions of students from across the globe learn in virtual classrooms, challenging the role and norms of educational institutions. In response to the global COVID-19 pandemic, school closings catapulted many educators and schools into online learning platforms. While these online universities and shifting remote classrooms are far from utopian, technology has changed and is likely to continue to change how education is delivered.

Not only has nearly every aspect of our lives been upended, but the world we live in today is faster, bigger, and more connected than at any other time in history. In 1965, Gordon Moore, one of the founders of Intel, wrote an article observing the complexity and speed of microprocessing development, and predicting that the number of transistors incorporated in a microchip will double every eighteen months. Remarkably,

Moore's law, as this axiom has become known, has continued to bear out for over fifty years. Memory chips today store approximately two billion times as much as they did when Moore made his prediction.

There are nearly eight billion people on planet Earth today, with over twenty-eight megacities of more than ten million people.[28] The public sector now serves nearly forty-three times the population it did at the turn of the twentieth century.[29] Writing in the *New Yorker*, Evan Osnos eloquently captured the sheer number of connected humans worldwide: "If Facebook were a country, it would have the largest population on Earth. More than 2.2 billion people, about a third of humanity, log in at least once a month."[30] Put differently, Facebook has as many adherents as Christianity.[31]

Technology has enabled an unprecedented scale of connection, action, and profit for the companies driving the U.S. economy. It used to take on average twenty years for a Fortune 500 company to become a billion-dollar business. Google did it in eight years. Facebook did it in five. Tesla did it in four. Uber did it in two and a half. The speed of growth and the financial size of these companies are unlike anything the world has seen before.[32]

In 1945, when the government undertook a major improvement effort to speed the delivery of mail from the United States to theaters of war in Europe, ordinary letters could take between twelve and twenty-three days to arrive.[33] Contrasted with the speed of communication today, when our inboxes overflow with e-mails and people find themselves simultaneously talking to coworkers across the globe on Slack, gchat, and Zoom, waiting two to three weeks for a letter seems practically comatose.

Governments and large institutions of all kinds are at a strategic disadvantage in a world where speed rules. Changing a policy, moving a bill, and appropriating funds have a speed and process all their own—one that has been largely unchanged for over a hundred years. When large institutions like government and technology collide, they often don't play nicely together. ELIS and many other government technology projects are built in multiyear government contracts with details baked into the fine print up front, while the pace of technology changes on a quarterly basis.

The U.S. government as we know it today is largely the result of massive federal expansions in the 1930s and the 1960s.[34] Imagine running an institution developed nearly 100 years ago in today's hyper-connected, fast-paced, constantly changing world. That is the fundamental challenge for the federal government.

Governments are not the only organizations enmeshed in the struggle to keep up. Nonprofits, universities, and large institutions like the United Nations or the World Health Organization face similar challenges. So does the private sector. Very few companies that were driving the economy at the turn of the twentieth century are leading the economy today. Of the Fortune 500 companies that made the list in 1955, only 20 percent are on the list today.[35] Kodak, for example, launched in 1888. For over 100 years, the company was the dominant household name in cameras. In the 1970s, Kodak sold 85 percent of film cameras and 90 percent of all film in the United States. They also invented the digital camera, but company executives didn't think it would take off, arguing that "no one would ever want to look at their pictures on a television set." In 2012, Kodak filed for bankruptcy.[36]

Failure Is Not an Option,
but Change Is Hard

Governments and public institutions don't have the prerogative to fail. Social Security is not going to be disrupted by an app called OldCash. People are not going to stop getting driver's licenses because the line at the DMV is too long. Governments and nonprofits must adapt to the modern world and find a way to deliver for the public. The U.S. government has been in service for hundreds of years with a similar structure. There is no competitor. There is no replacement.

Even more pressing, failure is not an option for the millions of people who rely on government for security, health, and safety. Sadly, as of this writing, in the United States we are seeing exactly what happens when government removes itself from the conversation. People who need access to food go hungry. People who need financial assistance and don't receive it get evicted. And in a public health crisis, a smattering of cases grows into a global pandemic, shuts down the economy, and leaves citizens sparring over the best way forward.

But if change is hard in the private sector, it is Sisyphean in government. In many parts of the private sector, a CEO can simply decide that a company will do something new. If the government wants to adapt its hiring practices to include higher salaries or modern benefits, it requires an act of Congress. This is true across developed democracies the world over. This feature alone makes keeping up with the speed of transformation a true challenge.

While technology is a driving factor in the transformation taking place, solving the intricately tangled problems of the modern age will require more than relying on an app or any single technology. It will require cultural shifts and new learning, skills, and tools. And though there is much to learn from the most cutting-edge practices in business, the work of meeting the world's challenges—tackling hunger, the climate crisis, inequality—is more complex than meeting those faced by the business world. Government and nonprofits cannot import techniques wholesale from the private sector without adapting them.

Up to Speed

Today, after many years of work, ELIS is functional. As of this writing, there are eight forms that can be processed through the system, which account for the majority of forms that come into USCIS.[37] In 2019 USCIS hired its first director of user experience, Michael Land, who made the switch from being a part of the USDS team to badge-carrying USCIS employee. Land is working toward incorporating research and design into the ELIS development process and bringing a consistent approach across the multiple contractor teams working on the project. IBM is no longer one of those teams. Some of the contractor teams consistently build prototypes (barebones working versions of the intended new functionality) and test them with users, then adjust their designs based on what they've learned. Some don't. Teams are still rated based on how fast they work rather than how well their product works.

"Change is very slow in government," says Land. "But we are moving in the right direction."[38]

2

Design, Data, and Delivery

INTRODUCING A NEW WAY of solving public problems and serving people is not a small enterprise. In this book, we focus on three key tools that have served the field well:

- Design: informed design that places humans at the center of the policy process
- Data: the use of real-time data to identify solutions and establish success metrics
- Delivery: focusing on delivery by running pilots before scaling

We will share three stories to illustrate what these tools look like in action, and introduce you to the people who made them happen. Our goal is to demonstrate how these methods allow nonprofits and governments to have an outsized impact on those they serve. These strategies are not the last word on problem solving. We're not even sure such a thing exists. But they will point you in the right direction.

It is also important to understand that these items aren't a create-your-own-salad menu that you can pick and choose from. You can't just do one and hope to effect real change. These are interlocking tools that, when taken together, form a model that seeks to have transformational impact. If you care about unraveling today's most intractable problems, you need to care about all three tools—design, data, and delivery.[1]

Design

The form that Detroit native Menica Harper faced was forty-two pages long, consisting of 18,409 words arranged into 1,204 questions.

"It was hell," said Harper.[2]

Harper had been through enough already. She had survived sexual assault and worked her way through mental health issues and chronic pain to become a home health aide, only to find herself homeless after her home burned in a fire. When she reached out to the state of Michigan for emergency help, she—like millions of Michiganders—was greeted with a nightmare of a form that stood between her and the assistance she needed for survival.

"It took me more than two hours to fill out," Harper said, "and I still got it wrong and left stuff out."[3]

Harper was wrestling with Form DHS-1171, the unified benefits application form. At the time it was the longest form for social assistance in the United States and the first barrier to entry for two million Michiganders seeking access to emergency assistance. Anyone in Michigan in dire need of healthcare, food assistance, emergency cash, or child care first needed to work their way through more than 1,200 questions.

This is no longer true.

The seeds for change were planted in 2011, thanks to one leader's obsession with the DHS-1171 form. Back then, Michael Brennan was the CEO of the United Way of Southeastern Michigan, one of the oldest and largest nonprofits in the United

States. In 2017 the organization raised $54 million to aid Michigan families—a colossal number for a regional nonprofit. Brennan started with the organization at age twenty-two and worked his way up over thirty-two years.

He came across the DHS-1171 form as part of a study the United Way had commissioned to map the social safety net—a term used for the combination of public benefits provided for families in need. The study revealed that funding the social safety net in Michigan at that time was a $35 billion enterprise, distributed between public (federal, state, and local) dollars and philanthropy. But even after the project was over, Brennan couldn't get Form DHS-1171 out of his mind. It was so onerous, so swollen with questions, and so very, very long.

"I carried that form around for six years," he told us.[4]

Brennan fashioned the form into a scroll by taping the pages together into more than forty feet of paper. He would roll it out in public meetings and events. He saw the form as the clearest evidence that the application and approval process for benefits in Michigan was not focused on the people it was intended to serve. The form repeated questions and asked parents to provide the date of conception for each child and whether there could be more than one potential father. At best, the questions were confusing and intrusive. At worst, they were humiliating.

"I gave a lot of speeches back then," Brennan recalls. "And I would hold it up as an example of how far we had gotten from trying to design things through the eyes of the person we're trying to serve, and how dominant the institution had become."[5]

Over time, Brennan came to believe that his field—the helping profession—was solving problems from the wrong angle. Too often, he saw, the user was missing—the very person his work was meant to help.

"In order to help the organization I was responsible for leading, and the wider community, I knew I had to do two things: unlearn ingrained methods of problem solving and open myself up to new ways. I knew I had to grow myself first before I could ever imagine helping others learn a new way of problem solving."[6]

In January 2014, at the age of fifty, Brennan took a leave of absence from the United Way to join a three-month residency at Stanford University's Hasso Plattner Institute of Design, known as the "D school." At Stanford, Brennan met Adam Selzer when he took Selzer's design leadership class. The two became fast friends after Brennan showed Selzer the DHS-1171 form over coffee. Selzer took it home to show Lena Selzer, a D school alumna and also his wife. In the form, the two of them saw the physical manifestation of an overly bureaucratic, bloated organization that had strayed from its public service roots.

"We had a hunch that the greatest way to scale positive change in society was through institutions, rather than on the edges, and that institutions felt enormous and very hard to change," Lena Selzer explains. "But if we could change them through human-centered design and other practices, there was a huge potential for impact. When Mike walked in with that application, it was such a good metaphor for that problem."[7]

In 2015, after completing his D school program, Brennan convinced the Selzers to move to Detroit and be his collaborators. The three started a nonprofit design studio called Civilla with the primary goal of changing the way public-serving institutions work. Civilla's first project was to improve the DHS-1171 form. Gabriela Dorantes had worked with Brennan at United Way, and eagerly joined the team as Civilla's first design researcher once she learned what the organization's approach would be. Dorantes had worked at nonprofits for years, but had recently experienced the same kind of lightbulb moment that Brennan and the Selzers had. She had come to the realization that any work that didn't incorporate user research was missing a significant piece of the puzzle.

"Obviously there were people that were talking directly to the users, but we, as the funders or program managers, that was not part of our process. I realized there are all these gaps that you fill based on what you've learned in school, or based on what you read, but not actually from people who are experiencing some of the things you're designing. And that blew my mind. I was like, wait, does everyone else know this?" Dorantes recalls.[8]

The Civilla team started by learning from the experiences of those who received food assistance, cash assistance, and Medicaid. In his decades at United Way, Brennan had established an extensive network of relationships with social advocates and organizations. The three Civilla founders tapped into those connections to find residents to meet with so they could learn firsthand what was working and what wasn't.

"Most of our time was in homes with residents, from ninety minutes to over two hours," Lena Selzer, cofounder and design director at Civilla, recalls of the early days.[9] They learned that for Michigan residents the process behind how applications were sorted and approved was as obtuse as the Hogwarts sorting hat.

"The system feels like a cosmic force. It feels like it's left up to fate whether you'll make it through," says Dr. La Tina Denson, one of the residents interviewed by the Civilla team as part of the original process.[10] A deeper look at the application data suggested that fate was perhaps a real factor—a lot of applications were being denied based purely on procedural reasons.

The Civilla team also began to understand the emotional and psychological states of applicants. Many felt the need to explain to Civilla researchers why they were in the position of needing benefits. Through the interviews, Dorantes began to see the form as almost inhumane.

"I had been doing nonprofit work, but to hear it directly from a person telling you: *I had this job, I have a college degree, I did everything right, and then this one thing happened.* And then this form is in the way, and they're having to justify why they're applying for benefits. It seemed really messed up. The reason that the safety net exists and why these benefits exist is for these reasons—you shouldn't feel ashamed or like you need to justify it or tell me how many degrees you have or that you tried to finish your degree," Dorantes says.[11]

After three months of collecting research, the Civilla team wanted to get their findings in front of someone who had the power to change things at the state level. They also wanted to build relationships with frontline state workers in order to better understand the system surrounding the form's processing. After a preliminary briefing with two officials from the Michigan Department of Health and Human Services (MDHHS) on their early research, MDHHS granted the Civilla team the connections with frontline workers they needed to complete their research. In turn, the Civilla team asked if they could brief a larger group of officials when their research was complete. This larger group of officials had no idea what they were in for.

Welcome to Tech Town

When MDHHS director Nick Lyon; Tim Becker, chief deputy director of the Michigan Department of Health and Human Services; Terry Beurer, senior deputy director of the Economic Stability Administration; and Rich Baird, a top aide to Governor Rick Snyder, arrived at Civilla's office for what they assumed was a routine briefing, they were surprised to discover that they were being treated (as authentically as possible) like applicants for the programs they oversaw.

The state officials were greeted at the elevator by Brennan. "Welcome to the DHS office of Tech Town," he said.

The officials were led to a noisy hallway lined with chairs and filled with other people also applying for benefits. They were given the DHS-1171 and told they had fifteen minutes to complete it. The environment was distracting, with people shuffling around and others in chairs filling out forms. It was also noisy. The Civilla team had taped office noise from a location where people were filling out the forms, and played it for the officials. After an awkward fifteen minutes, the Civilla team told the officials their time was up. None of the officials had finished the application in the allotted time.

Several of the officials had never seen the form up close. While that may be hard to imagine, this type of distance is commonplace across government. The farther up the hierarchy a person gets, the more distance they have from both the people they serve and the caseworkers who serve them. This is in part because the rules that govern leaders are anchored in compliance with state and federal laws. Health and human services leaders, for example, are often called in by the governor to make sure they are staying within budget or are prepared for an outbreak or disease. They are often asked to brief state legislators on their pet priorities. There is less of a demand that they focus on the people at the receiving end. While this is theoretically everyone's job, it is often one of thousands of duties. Public sector workers and states face serious penalties for giving someone a benefit who shouldn't have received one. Conversely, no one gets a trophy or a raise for enrolling more people in a benefit, speeding the process, or simplifying people's lives.[12]

After they had completed the application simulation, the Civilla team walked the visiting officials through a 100-foot journey map of what happens to an application after it leaves an applicant's hands. While the officials studied the journey map, the team shared the stories of civil servants working at MDHHS to help officials understand the application process in context. At the end of the meeting, the team presented the state officials with a prototype of a new form. This new version was built around ideas and recommendations from potential beneficiaries and state workers that Civilla had gathered at community design sessions. The prototype was a vision of how things could be.

That unconventional meeting was the beginning of Civilla's partnership with MDHHS. Dorantes thinks that one of the factors that contributed to the success of what is now called "the exhibit" (which is preserved and can be visited in the Civilla offices) is that it generated an understanding of all sides of the application process, including not only applicants but civil servants, whose dedication to public service made the existing form's failings more apparent.

"The [civil servants] that I met, they're some of the most amazing, lovely people who were called to public service because they wanted to contribute to their community. So you start to wonder, what is the disconnect? Because there are people on the other side processing these applications who really do want to help," Dorantes said. "What's unique about [the exhibit] is that you are acknowledging how both sides are feeling and you are asking people to step into it and make their own judgment. Here are both sides of the story. What do you think about that?"[13]

What MDHHS thought about it was immediately apparent. The agency committed that day to work to improve the application process.

Building a Prototype

The teams decided to run a pilot in two MDHHS offices, offering a small slice of potential beneficiaries a new, easier to use application. But first, they had to create a model application that complied with the law. Nearly 1,700 pages of rules and regulations governed the five benefit programs that accepted the application. Lena Selzer describes these regulations as the project team's first Mount Everest—to get their aspirational prototype to align with reality, the team first had a mountain of rules to climb.

Because the Civilla team was not fluent in HHS policy, they worked side by side with policy experts from different departments in MDHHS. After six months of work and lots of support for tough decisions from the department's leadership, the joint team produced a viable test application that both complied with the rules and was accessible to the average Michigander.

(Note that in this chapter we are very frank about the amount of work and time that goes into these efforts. We are not encouraging anyone to move fast and break things. It took a full year from when Civilla and the state agreed to fix the form for the project to start. Projects that successfully incorporate user-centered design, data, and testing take time. Doing things right the first time takes time. But the time saved on not creating something disastrous or useless is immeasurable.)

The application tests went well. The time to finish the application was down to about twenty minutes from the usual forty-five, and fewer people were quitting before they reached the end. After another few rounds of fixes and a collaboration to develop training for using the new form, the team began slowly replacing the old form with the newer, shorter version.

What began as a test for a small group of clients and caseworkers was improved and—after extensive training with over 5,000 field staff across 100 offices—brought statewide to 2.5 million residents. The entire project had taken 813 days, but the new form was 80 percent shorter, and state workers were able to process it in half the time of the old form. Most users now complete the form in less than twenty minutes. Submitted applications are 94 percent complete the first time people fill them out, making a real difference for the frontline caseworkers.

"I feel like I can breathe again," said one applicant after completing the form. "It was so simple, it made me feel comfortable."[14]

"The old application would have taken me a whole day," another Michigan resident said. "This one was more understandable and less stressful. It asks you the questions but with respect."[15]

Civilla isn't alone. Their collaborative work with the state of Michigan is among several threads of similar collaboration on benefits integration, including with Vermont, a story we share later in this chapter, and three other states. The ultimate goal for Civilla is to have applicants apply and be approved on the same day.

Success Relies on Building Empathy

The Civilla team attributes a large portion of their success to the way they brought MDHHS into the project in that first meeting. Taking officials through the application in a realistic way not only built empathy on the part of leadership, but it brought everyone's focus squarely on the form's users. Having attempted to fill out the form themselves, the leadership couldn't help but think of the people who would be affected every time a policy or regulation meant lengthening the form.

"None of [this] would have occurred if we went up to Lansing and shared our set of insights on a slide deck," says Brennan. "When we took the risk to have them sit out in the hallway with a bunch of other people and have them fill out the forty-two-page application before we even talked to them, all of that gives permission to a leader to arrive as more than their full selves."[16]

This kind of empathy-building approach has been used around the globe to great effect. Kit Collingwood, a digital government leader in the UK, notes that "higher-empathy policy making practice leads to better policy, which leads to better services, which leads to efficiency and cost savings, as well as happier people out there in the real world."[17]

DJ Patil, former chief data scientist for the United States, describes using compassion as "a better approach to actually do things." Compassion, to Patil, effectively teams up "user experience, and data, and people who are experts in the system. All that has to come together."[18]

Build with, Not for

The Civilla team purposefully included end users in the design process, which guaranteed that the final form would meet applicants where they were.

"I feel like this is the first project that got designed at a field level," said one MDHHS caseworker. "It's not just what the leaders in Lansing want. I appreciate all the input I've been able to provide."[19]

The DHS-1171 form redesign project began and ended with people. The focus on understanding both beneficiaries and frontline state workers grounded the team's efforts. Hearing how the process wasn't working for anyone helped make the case for change.

Bringing a user-centered approach to projects via relentless research into users' behavior, likes, and motivations is the lifeblood of many of the more successful products we know and love. The Civilla team spent hundreds of hours interviewing applicants and frontline workers to make sure the form was accessible and easy to use while also answering the questions

Michigan needed to process applications. That might sound like a lot of research for one form, but it pales in comparison to private sector efforts. A well-known financial services company tested the name of a single navigation item on their site with 455 participants using a prototype. The same site has also run tests on whether menus should fade in or appear all at once, as well as large-scale usability and eye tracking studies on whether donut or pie charts are easier to read. Overall, the team conducts hundreds of user experience research studies every year, often with over 1,000 participants in a single study.[20]

Understanding users isn't an activity that is limited to Fortune 500 companies or Silicon Valley start-ups who have happened into a pile of money. Fields from community organizing to anthropology undertake this work as a routine part of their disciplines. But while understanding the people you are serving makes sense, it is not a practice that is central to how many of our institutions are built. In most government agencies different teams see different aspects of program data and are siloed from the full service landscape. One team oversees call centers, another oversees the website, another works with caseworkers. It is no single person's job to look across channels at the overall experience interacting with the agency and see "customers."

Build with, Not for . . . Even if You Are Building Technology

Focusing on users is a core principle for multiple entities that have been established to bring technology expertise to government. The Government Digital Service (GDS) in the United Kingdom, Code for America (CfA),[21] and USDS[22] have all published works and guidelines that start with focusing on what people need.

Todd Park, the first chief technology officer (CTO) at Health and Human Services, and former White House CTO, says that in his work across the federal government, the goal of helping users often got lost in projects that were focused on technology. So his team would work to bring the focus back to users. Park explains that the benefit of thinking in a user-, citizen-, and customer-centered way goes far beyond making software easier to use.

"The benefit of a user-centered mindset is incredibly helpful to have in government of any kind, whether it involves tech or not," he explains.[23]

Park saw that agencies that incorporated user-centered design for tech products would also start to use the approach on other projects, incorporating a culture of seeking input from users across the agency. After doing deep user design on one project within the Department of Education, Park said he'd heard the agency had sent a USDS staffer out to talk to students on the Washington Mall about their needs before rolling out a new regulation.

————

While user experience is a field in its own right, populated by people with deep expertise, it is also a mindset anyone can bring to a project. Deducing that filling out a form with 1,800 questions will be an onerous experience doesn't require a design degree from Stanford. By starting and ending with the people the form aimed to serve, along with the civil servants who would be processing the form, the Civilla team was able to chip away at the form's length question by question. Collaboration with institutional leaders like those inside MDHHS and with external resources such as those provided by Civilla made possible what no one organization could do alone.

Many others around the world have observed that government cannot continue in its current state, and new collaborations to empower organizations to design with users are cropping up. UK social activist and 2005 Designer of the Year Hilary Cottam has started large-scale social experiments in the UK using design thinking. Cottam describes the need to upgrade institutional design: "What is important is that we make our systems regenerative so they work for humans and our natural world. The types of problems we face require the engagement and participation of citizens to solve—we cannot change our consumption patterns or our health by being told to do so. We need to ask again what people really need to flourish, and we need to work in a different way, with people."[24]

In the Civilla story we've highlighted how the team focused on users and redesigned a system. It is important to note that the team also used data and pilots to refine and test their ideas. In the next section we'll take a more detailed look at what it means to use data effectively.

Data

One day in 2009, Stephanie Shih, a staffer at DoSomething.org—an organization dedicated to getting young people to engage in more service and civic actions via reminders and texts—was sending mass texts about opportunities to volunteer to thousands of people when she received an unexpected series of texts back:

"He won't stop raping me . . .

"It's my dad . . .

"He told me not to tell anyone. . . .

"R U there?"[25]

Too afraid to call or speak to anyone, this young person in crisis had anonymously texted a complete stranger for help. It would occasionally happen that people would send texts to Do-Something.org about being bullied, or about a friend with addiction. But there was no protocol for something like this. Stephanie stayed connected to the anonymous texter, shared resources for RAINN (Rape, Abuse & Incest National Network), and encouraged her to seek help. But the rape victim said she was too scared to call.

Stephanie printed out the texts and brought them to her boss, Nancy Lublin, the CEO of DoSomething.org. Lublin couldn't get them out of her mind. The texts inspired her to found Crisis Text Line, an organization aimed at reaching young people in crisis via a place they already knew well—their phones. Lublin says simply, "We built Crisis Text Line for her."[26]

This young woman wasn't alone. Her reticence to use the phone is shared by millions. Her obstacles to seeking help are also obstacles for many others—a generation in crisis that won't pick up the phone or seek help in person. Text is their language, where they live, and how they connect. There are 277 million texters in the United States.[27] The average eighteen- to-twenty-four-year-old sends 128 texts a day, nearly double that of the next age cohort up.[28] For 37 percent of the people who reach out to Crisis Text Line, it is the first time they are reaching out for support from anyone.[29]

Crisis Text Line's core public health intervention isn't new. Across the country there are hundreds of 1-800 phone lines serving people with different issues, among them suicide, eating disorders, and sexual abuse. Many are run by local governments and nonprofits. The federal government, too, funds this work, and has for decades. But Crisis Text Line brought 1-800 numbers into the digital age with two improvements: they could be accessed via text, and they would not be issue-specific—anyone in any kind of crisis could reach out anytime.

At first the organization sought to build a text service for existing crisis help centers to use. They began by building, testing, and monitoring a twenty-four-hour text line in Chicago and El Paso, where texters could reach trained counselors at existing crisis centers. Within months, they were fielding texts from every zip code in the continental United States. In order to meet the needs of this growing number of texters, the team needed to bring on more trained counselors. But first, they gathered feedback on their existing counselors by asking texters to fill out a survey after their text exchanges. In reviewing the surveys, the team found that the quality of counseling varied wildly across both crisis centers and individual counselors. To improve the quality of counseling, they decided to launch their own volunteer operation, and Crisis Text Line was born.

Here's how the service works today: When a person in need texts Crisis Text Line, no matter the time of day, Crisis Text Line will text them back with an automated response including a data privacy agreement and the question "What's your crisis?" The texters' responses are then sorted by an algorithm, which also ensures that texts containing words like "I want to die" are coded as high-risk and moved to the front of the queue. Texters are then able to begin a real-time conversation with a counselor, usually within five minutes for those classified as high-risk.

The goal, from Crisis Text Line's perspective, is to bring people to a cooler place using evidence-based practices from the counseling field. During the course of a text conversation, Crisis Text Line counselors are supported by algorithms, and their responses and work are observed closely by trained clinical supervisors. All volunteer counselors work remotely, but they are supervised in real time by a staff member with master's level experience in social work or psychology. The bar to become a counselor is high. Counselors must first complete thirty

hours of training and undergo a background check and reference checks in order to qualify. Only about 30 percent of applicants make it. But the flexibility of volunteering remotely has
enabled a deep level of engagement from nearly a thousand
volunteers who log on each day.

The volume of texts varies hour by hour and day by day, and
often reflects world events. On Election Night 2016 the service
experienced four times their standard call volume. The week of
Kate Spade's and Anthony Bourdain's suicides there was a
116 percent increase in text volume over the previous week.

But even on an average day the service's reach is impressive.
On the day we visited Crisis Text Line's headquarters in New
York City, they'd had 3,152 conversations over the previous
twenty-four hours. In the same time period New York City's 911
line averages 4,000 calls.[30] Crisis Text Line's work has a huge
footprint. In six years, they have been part of 129 million messages, over 50,000 suicide de-escalations, and more than 30,000
active rescues.

Through texts, they have met and helped underserved populations who are often beyond the reach of traditional mental
health organizations. Seventy-five percent of their texters are
under the age of twenty-five. Nineteen percent are Latinx.
Nearly half identify as LGBTQ. Almost a quarter come from
some of the lowest income zip codes in the country.[31]

Learning in Real Time

This volume of data produces a treasure trove of information.
Unlike phone conversations or clinical sessions, which would
need to be recorded and transcribed in order to be analyzed for
trends, Crisis Text Line's data is automated and collected in real
time as texts happen. The sheer number of texts and texters

enables learning that would not be possible with data collected from a single crisis center, and provides real-time data about the pain people are feeling and how they express it.

The nation's largest stores of mental health data come from surveys from the Centers for Disease Control and Prevention (CDC) and the National Institutes of Health (NIH). But these surveys ask people to respond to prompts months after the fact (e.g., Have you had suicidal thoughts in the last year?). This creates what scientists refer to as recency bias, a phenomenon whereby people remember and recount things that happened more recently, not months before. There is also a lag in data collection and publication, as the federal data is published well over a year after being collected.

Bob Filbin, Crisis Text Line's cofounder and chief data scientist, points out that the CDC and NIH surveys are written by scientists, which by default means that scientists are the ones drawing the boundaries of what qualifies as a crisis.

"Our data starts from the opposite direction, allowing the users to define what crisis looks like to them. The survey questions need to be complemented with data collection that allows users to express their voice outside of predefined buckets. That's what we do. We can see how crisis changes by day and location in a way that others can't," says Filbin.[32]

Real-Time Data Is Knowledge, and Knowledge is Power

By analyzing their data, Crisis Text Line has learned which times of day people are most vulnerable, what types of words present a higher risk for suicide, and which communities or age groups might be facing acute challenges that are not otherwise captured by existing forms of data on mental health.

For example, the team has learned which words are more likely to lead to high-risk conversations. Interestingly, those conversations don't necessarily contain the word "suicide." Instead, the emoji for a pill is 4.4 times more likely to result in a life-threatening situation. Words about pills are sixteen times more likely to result in a call to 911 than the words "suicide" or "overdose." Even more startling, the word "military' is two times more likely than the word "suicide" to predict suicide. It is this sort of knowledge that provides a very valuable tool for counselors who are trying to determine if a texter is just going through a bad breakup or is close to harming themselves.

Analyzing the timing and content from texts has also helped the organization identify times of day when issues peak. They've found that conversations around depression peak at 8 p.m., while those related to anxiety peak at 11 p.m., those about self-harm at 4 a.m., and those about substance abuse at 5 a.m.

Crisis Text Line's data doesn't only identify words that predict harm, but also words that build resilience. According to the organization's data scientists, the words "brave," "smart," and "proud" are most associated with strength identification. Having counselors use phrases like "it was brave of you to reach out" or "I am so proud of you for seeking counseling" can help texters identify their own strengths.[33]

Crisis Text Line has also applied their data-based learning internally to improve how their counseling arm functions. When the organization learned that 4 a.m. was a high-risk time of day, they recruited more counselors to cover this time. After learning that informal language is more effective with texters, and that contractions like "can't" instead of "cannot" seemed to work better, Crisis Line rewrote their training and coaching materials to suggest that counselors use an informal approach to better build trust and connection.

With Great Power Comes Great Responsibility

Crisis Text Line's data can do a world of good. The data enabled sex workers to free themselves from captivity. Really. But it can also be misused. As we were finishing this book, the complexities and risks inherent in this type of data work were laid bare. Nancy Lubin, the former CEO, was removed by the board of directors in response to accusations from staff of a hostile work environment. Among the extensive list of charges from former staff were issues with her management style and the organization's culture; a pattern of racial insensitivity; and questionable use of how Lubin requested, read, and interpreted data.[34] Crisis Text Line collects demographic data in order to improve the recruiting and training of a diverse cohort of counselors to serve their equally diverse clientele. That data was allegedly misused by Lubin when she requested to see counselors' productivity rates by race.

Data can be used to help see implicit biases, or it can amplify pervasive inequalities and power dynamics that may be embedded in organizational structures. A precondition of doing this work is the ability to see beyond the data to the people. To us, the unfolding story of Crisis Text Line illustrates the maxim (variants of which are attributed to both Winston Churchill and Spiderman) that with great power comes great responsibility.

In part because of the potential for harm, the Crisis Text Line data team works under the watch of a high-power data advisory board.[35] The team maintains that they take data collection, storing, and privacy very seriously. The organization divides their data work into four key areas—security, privacy, and confidentiality; analysis; use of data; and partnerships—the last of which is crucial because it governs the controlled sharing of data.

But a missing pillar of the data agenda is *equity*. It is possible that a greater level of diversity in Crisis Text Line's leadership would have prevented some of their data blind spots and sped action on staff concerns. We will discuss the risks involved in data, and how data and diversity intersect in especially important ways in the public interest technology space, later in this book. For now, it is enough to know that using real data to understand how you are serving people is a very powerful tool, but it is also a reflection of the people using it—with positive and negative implications.

Delivery

For many years the de facto way to build a massive new system was to build it in one fell swoop, then hit the on switch. Over the past ten years or so, the private sector has—company by company—adjusted to the idea that this is perhaps not the best way to run most projects. One report found that as of 2019, 97 percent of companies around the world reported using agile in some capacity, though that data is self-reported and so should be taken with a brick-sized grain of salt.[36]

As we discussed in the last chapter, the public sector, like the private sector, is still making this change. Even as we wrote this book, examples of the danger of building a midsized thing and hitting the on switch were piling up across both government and the private sector. A debacle involving the 2020 Iowa caucus, where a poorly designed app layered on top of a poorly designed process meant that the Democratic caucus results were delayed by weeks, was the year's first example. The day of the Iowa caucus, one of us was in a private hospital awaiting surgery, only to learn that the hospital had that very day switched over to a new patient management system. The switch meant that surgeries were delayed for hours and left doctors unable to prescribe some anesthetics or needed drugs for an entire day. While it didn't make the headlines the way that a public sector disaster might, the company's tech failure was a disaster for thousands of doctors, nurses, and patients.

Sometimes people in government say the words "we are running a pilot," but in reality these "pilots" look more like massive soft launches (a soft launch is a lightly announced or hush-hush rollout of a new technology), with multicity efforts and limited data collection. One of us was brought in to consult on a government "pilot" that had been running for six months in a static state, processing hundreds of people per day as they boarded international flights. The other worked in the White House on the rollout and recovery of Healthcare.gov, which launched nationwide without any soft launch or live testing for a small set of users. The goal of a pilot should always be to see how a new process, system, or technology works in real life, to make adjustments accordingly, and then test those adjustments.

Start Small, Learn, Improve, and Scale

The Integrated Benefits Initiative, a joint project between Code for America, the Center on Budget and Policy Priorities, and Nava Public Benefit Corporation, is a big idea kind of endeavor, driven by the desire to build an equitable, human-centered safety net for the digital age. All states are responsible for administering their own federally funded programs, such as free or low-cost healthcare and assistance paying for food. Because the programs are administered at the state level, they are implemented in fifty different ways, with fifty different user experiences. In some states the process is entirely paper based. In Michigan, as we just shared, applicants used to fill out the lon-

gest form in the country. The idea behind the Integrated Benefits Initiative is to start making things easier and more equitable
for applicants by picking a handful of states and improving how
residents access these critical benefits.

But even big ideas must start small. The team involved in
getting Healthcare.gov to function had glimpsed the potential
to build on the technological advances that Healthcare.gov ultimately brought to government, such as automating real-time
approvals for Medicaid applicants. What if, they thought, we
could also simplify the way families apply for other services,
like food or financial or housing assistance? For the team at U.S.
Health and Human Services (HHS), which had overseen the
administration of Healthcare.gov, all of these services were
intertwined. Modernizing the way approvals worked for healthcare was merely the first step. With the change in administration in 2016, the HHS team wanted to ensure that the thread of
the work wasn't lost. So they took the idea to Nava Public Benefits Corporation, a public interest technology company built
by veterans of the Healthcare.gov recovery, and CfA.[37] Nava
and CfA, in turn, were able to get philanthropic funding to pilot
a new way of applying for benefits in five different states.

The team conducted exploratory field research in seven
states before they found one to sign on to their idea. Some
states weren't interested; others wanted to sign on but couldn't
get the departmental or regulatory wheels turning fast enough.
But the team had a good feeling about Vermont as soon as they
met with Cass Madison, Vermont's deputy commissioner for
the Department of Vermont Health Access.

This work always requires strong leadership at the top, someone who gives permission for an organization to take risks and
fail.[38] It also always relies on the expertise and dedication of
frontline civil servants to make things function. And as we have

already noted, this work is tough, and it takes time. (We are really selling it, aren't we?)

"You had better want this more than anything else, for the leader and the organization that is trying to help," Michael Brennan told us about powering Civilla's work in Michigan.[39] When the Nava team first met Cass Madison, they could tell immediately that she wanted this more than anything else.

Madison had seen firsthand what had happened with Vermont's efforts to establish a health exchange. In 2012 she was working on the policy side of government when she was brought in to help stand up Vermont Health Connect, the state's ACA-mandated health insurance marketplace.

"I had a front row seat to the challenges that we experienced during that time with the launch of Vermont Health Connect and saw what not to do, essentially, standing up a new piece of technology like that. As things got worse, I just ended up jumping in operationally to help stabilize things and then jumped in on the technology side to help stabilize the technology," Madison told us.[40]

By the time Nava met with Madison she had already reached out to CfA and18F, a federal agency that offers support on digital services and technology projects, for help rethinking not only the state's road map, but their practices around project management, procurement, and software development. She'd concluded that Vermont could not keep doing projects the way they had been, with large multiyear multimillion-dollar waterfall contracts and antiquated design techniques. The Integrated Benefits Initiative was the opportunity Madison had been looking for.

"It was this aha moment," Madison recalls. "All of these things that I had felt intuitively, now all of a sudden I realized there was a language and a practice and a process around."[41]

Madison's excitement about working with Nava trickled down to her team as well. Thani Boskailo, who worked under Madison as Vermont's healthcare director of operations, had also been through the torturous launch of Vermont Health Connect, but her entire demeanor brightens when talking about the Integrated Benefits Initiative.

"Everyone was trying to do things this one way, this old way, but here is a new way and we're going to figure it out—we're going to be the ones who solve the problem that people for close to a decade have been trying to figure out, and we're going to make Vermonters' lives easier," Boskailo recalls. "It was exciting. When you think you're on the brink of major change to make everybody's lives better, it's an adrenaline rush. We were doing what other states hadn't figured out yet. We were doing what our state hadn't figured out yet. Vermont is known for being progressive. And here we were getting that opportunity to do that."[42]

After working together to stabilize Vermont Health Connect, Boskailo and Madison were eager to take on a new challenge. As Boskailo recalls, "Here we were after we had solved that problem, thinking, 'Hey we can make it even better.' And [Madison] said, 'I want you by my side, just like we were with our healthcare operations. We can do it.'"[43]

———

Vermont is a state laced with winding two-lane roads, with long distances between towns and a spine-like mountain range in the middle of the state. Driving around Vermont calls to mind nearby Maine's turn of phrase, "You can't get there from here." In Vermont, the shortest distance between two points is often a squiggle. Which made the state's antiquated system for applying for state benefits particularly arduous.

Applications for nearly everything needed to be submitted in person at a field office. Applicants would then return to the office for an interview if one couldn't be scheduled immediately. And then again with supporting documentation, which could either be mailed in or hand delivered. A significant number of applicants chose to drop off the documents rather than risk possibly losing them to the Postal Service. Offices were only open during standard business hours, which meant that if someone had a full-time job in another town they would be unlikely to make it to the benefits field office without taking time off from work. And given the long stretches of countryside between Vermont towns and limited public transportation options, applying without a car was nearly impossible.

The integrated benefits team had a hypothesis that submitting applications online would save people a lot of time and hassle. But rather than initiate a massive contract to overhaul the benefits application, the Nava team knew they wanted to start small, having already lived through big public sector launches that didn't go so well. So rather than proposing a project that would integrate all benefits programs into a single application, which would mean not only working across business units but also working across old systems that, as Genevieve Gaudet, a program manager at Nava, put it, might be "in a closet somewhere," they started with a twelve-week project.[44]

By the end of the twelve weeks, the plan was for the team to have built and tested a prototype that allowed a small group of Vermonters to upload eligibility documentation online for a single benefit program: SNAP—the Supplemental Nutrition Assistance Program, also known as food stamps. The prototype would provide enough information for decision makers in Vermont on whether this was something they wanted to implement statewide.

The team chose to start with SNAP because they knew that in order to qualify for SNAP, applicants must do an interview, either over the phone or in person. The interview was a built-in touch-point between the applicant and a caseworker, which meant that a human could introduce the new tool to applicants. The team wouldn't need to make any big process changes to run the pilot. Additionally, all of the economic services in Vermont are administered at the district office level, dividing applicants between twelve different districts. SNAP is an economic service, so starting there automatically gave the team a small sample size to test with, without disrupting larger-scale operations. Keeping the pilot at one office also reduced the number of people who needed to be trained on how to use the new tool. Rather than train an airplane hangar's worth of call center reps, the team only needed to train one field office's caseworkers. While the tool needed to make applying for programs easy for Vermonters, it also needed to make it easy for frontline staff to support Vermonters.

Finally, one of the huge benefits to biting off a very small chunk of a project was that the team could stay small and move quickly, as they didn't need to get buy-in from statewide decision makers, business units, or funding owners. Because they weren't building a giant permanent entity for all Vermonters, the team was able to delay conversations on complex topics like how to build a login system that would authenticate the entire state population's identity. For the pilot, the focus would simply be on testing whether submitting a single form online made life easier or harder for all involved.

The team also had clear internal goals as to what the tool they were building should achieve in order to be worth scaling statewide. The plan was to have fifty people use the new tool, measure how things went, and then decide if they wanted to turn it off or let it keep running.

All pilots need to start in a physical place, even virtual pilots. The team met with people in a number of the twelve district offices across the state before settling on the office in Barre (pronounced bare-ee). In a state with a lot of wide-open empty spaces, Barre qualifies as a booming metropolis, with 9,000 residents and a restored but rickety nineteenth-century opera house. The town is home to one of the world's largest granite quarries, in operation since the 1800s, but like many of the Northeast's mining areas Barre has seen better days, and the main street is a mixture of adorable restaurants and boarded-up storefronts. Which led us to wonder if perhaps the Nava team chose Barre because the town has a high percentage of SNAP applicants.

"No," Gaudet quickly corrected. "It's because they had Jimmy."[45]

Successful innovation projects require at least one person on the inside who is clued in to proposed changes, even excited by them—a person who will open doors instead of slamming them shut and barricading them with stacks of office furniture, red tape, and unanswered e-mails. Jimmy Crisante had already gotten his field office to experiment with having applicants e-mail documents, which technically was against the rules. He was exactly the kind of bureaucrat the Nava team needed.

"We had a champion in that office," Gaudet notes. "And that was the thing that set the office apart as a good place for us to start."[46]

The team also knew they wanted to be able to track whether the new tool was faster than the old tool, but Vermont didn't have metrics on their current system. So they gathered metrics manually by sitting side by side with a case manager in a district office.

Domenic Fichera, a product manager at Nava, describes his week working together with Crisante in the Barre office, figuring out how long it took SNAP applicants to be approved from the time they submitted their applications. Fichera explains the process used: "He and I went through fifty cases, and I asked, 'When did this person submit their application? When did they have their interview? When did we ask them to submit documents? When did their documents arrive? And when did they receive their eligibility outcome?' I wrote those dates down in a spreadsheet for each of these fifty people. And then that's how we calculated our baseline."[47]

This also helped the team settle on the correct size of the pilot. If they could manually page through fifty people's paper applications for SNAP, maybe they could work to get fifty people to submit their documents electronically for SNAP.

"Everything Is Working Perfectly"

To run the pilot they built a small form and a document uploader tool that would allow fifty applicants to send their documentation to the state while they were on the phone with a caseworker in the Barre office. The team ran a training for workers in Barre—all four caseworkers in the office went through it—which included talking points for uploading documents with the form, and how to respond to objections.

In part because the Barre office had been involved in the research—the Nava team spent significant time observing caseworkers' interviews and understanding their day-to-day operations—the office was excited to participate in the pilot. They saw that digital uploading was going to make not only their lives easier but also the lives of the applicants they ushered through the system. As noted earlier, one of the widely espoused tenets of this work is "Build with, not for," which is exactly what the Vermont benefits team did by working so closely with Crisante, caseworkers, and Vermonters in designing how the tool should work. Once it came time to pilot the tool, this "with, not for" culture paid the team back with caseworkers who were excited and eager to try something new.

When it came time to start the pilot, the Nava team released the small form and the uploader tool and allowed caseworkers to route applicants to it. While the workers were conducting their SNAP interviews over the phone, they listed which documents the Vermonters needed to provide, per usual. Then, they asked people if they would like to send the documents electronically. If applicants said yes, they became a part of the pilot. The caseworker would direct them to a special test URL that allowed the applicants to submit their documents online. The caseworker could then confirm, in real time, that the documents had been received.

It took about a month of this process to reach the goal of fifty test cases. The impact of the pilot was immediately apparent. Previously, the end-to-end process—from asking for documents to receiving an approval or rejection—took nine days, not to mention the number of car trips involved to retrieve missing documents.

"We ask for a lot of documentation," Crisante told the Nava team. "If we ask someone to send A, B, and C, we usually end up receiving B, part of C, and F."[48]

During the pilot, applicants who submitted their documents electronically saw their wait time cut in half, down from nine days to four and a half. No car needed. Best of all, of the applicants who used the electronic uploader, 55 percent received a determination within twenty-four hours. Previously, same-day determinations happened for a paltry 6 percent of applicants. Interestingly, 40 percent of applicants used the uploader outside of office hours, confirming the team's hypothesis that the Barre office's hours were making it difficult for applicants to submit their documents.

By keeping everything small, from the team size to the product being tested, Vermont was able to clarify the best way forward in a small amount of time with very little risk, very little disruption to the people staffing the Barre office, and no disruption to Vermonters.

"A team of four or five of us on the Nava side—for a pretty small amount of money—in twelve weeks, were able to validate and put a bunch of data behind why providing a tool like this would provide extreme value to the state and to Vermonters before they invested in big complex integrations and updates to their reporting structure," says Fichera. "It was a great proof of concept."[49]

On the government side, the Vermont team was thrilled with the outcome, and together with Nava they agreed it should be rolled out statewide. Even with the positive numbers, selling the new product statewide required a significant effort. Madison, Gaudet, and others presented the pilot findings to the Vermont legislature in order to get the state budget to include rolling out the uploader statewide. To explain the new uploader tool to a room full of legislators, the team let each member try the tool out themselves. In what was likely a first for the state's legislative body, the team handed out fake pay stubs and asked people to take pictures with their phones and upload them into the system.

"The idea was, let's stop telling people what we're going to do and let's actually show them what we're doing," Madison recalled. "I think that was incredibly powerful. People were very excited. We were able to have all of the discussions by showing them what this actually looked like. Then we talked to them about what the process was like. What does prototyping look like? How do we iterate? We showed them a picture of the very first prototype, which was just a hand-drawn design."[50]

Because Vermont had been through bad technology launches, the plan was not to terrify anyone, to be reassuring, and to move softly.

"We needed to be very careful and make this slow and measured case like, 'It's safe to adopt this, this is not going to bring down any programs. You're not going to have crazy backlogs or calls to your constituent offices as a result of this technology not working,'" Fichera says.[51]

Immediately after the pilot, the team worked to have the documents applicants uploaded go directly to the existing document management system, removing a step for caseworkers. That pilot started in the Barre office too, in part because the Barre team had been so welcoming the first time around.

"Once that happened, it was almost eerie. I didn't hear anything. I called Jimmy to check in. He's like, 'Yeah, it's smooth, the only reason we didn't reach out is because there were no issues at all, everything is working perfectly.' And we're like, that's amazing," Fichera says.[52]

The uploader was rolled out statewide for SNAP, and then expanded to include applications for healthcare. Because the online application would take the place of a whole suite of applications with different security and policy regulations, it ran the risk of being mired in regulatory hell for years. To avoid that outcome, the team continued to take small steps. The state's road map for the entire integrated benefits project spanned five years, with the next step being creating an online customer portal that would serve as a one-stop shop for Vermonters' benefits applications.

In October 2019, Nava began by building the very first piece of the portal—an electronic version of the paper form for Medicaid applications for the aged, blind, and disabled. The team knew that these Vermonters had no electronic options at all when it came to applying for Medicaid and that the process could take a very long time. The idea was that after the Medicaid application launched, it would serve as a foundational layer for the rest of the portal.

By starting small and working in iterative steps throughout Vermont's benefits forms, the state was able to tackle what otherwise could have felt like a very overwhelming, daunting, and expensive project. But running a tiny twelve-week pilot with a form, an uploader, and fifty people on the phone outside of a mining town felt doable.

The concept of starting small and scaling has already been embraced by some teams in the public sector. The UK's GDS design principles espouse the value of starting small and iterating "wildly": "Release minimum viable products early, test them with actual users, move from alpha to beta to live adding features, deleting things that don't work and making refinements based on feedback. Iteration reduces risk. It makes big failures unlikely and turns small failures into lessons. If a prototype isn't working, don't be afraid to scrap it and start again."[53]

The Vermont team spent a lot of time figuring out where to start, even with the limitations they had imposed upon themselves. We have seen this struggle play out in our own work too. In a project with a large city that one of us worked on, figuring out where to start took six months, followed by over a year of legal wrangling. In other projects, figuring out where to start can seem so overwhelming that it feels easier to just call in a contractor or to throw the whole project out the window. But by thinking about these projects not as large monolithic entities but as small test scenarios ("Let's try this! Let's try that!"), they can not only feel more feasible but also have the benefit of providing immediate, measurable results.

Civilla's Michael Brennan argues that starting small has an even greater value when it comes to finding a way into intractable problems.

Says Brennan, "One of our observations is these systems that don't work for anybody, they all have a front door and that front door needs a key in order to get in. For example, on a public benefits system, you can't get in that door unless you have a completed application. It has a disproportionate effect in some ways as a gateway to the wider and larger system."[54]

It can sometimes take time to find the right key in the heavy tangle of a government key ring, which calls to mind perhaps the largest collection of keys ever held together, some as old as skeleton keys and others that use the Ring app. There will be projects that are too big or too risky or too complicated. There will be agencies that are too slow or contentious to work with. But ultimately, for those tenacious enough to keep trying, the right project will appear, and it will be the key that opens the front door.

Not So Fast: When Public Interest Technology Fails

The story of the Vermont benefits work has an important coda.

Nava's work with Vermont didn't only involve small, incremental builds. It also involved small, incremental procurements. With the uploader and the Medicaid application complete, Nava submitted a bid to expand the online application. Two weeks later, while the team was still waiting to hear back on the next piece of work, the pandemic hit.

With buildings closed and people quarantined at home, the uploader, which previously had served as a test piece of technology, became indispensable. Usage jumped from a few hundred users to over 3,000 a month. But the state of Vermont, like so many others, found itself struggling to stay afloat operationally with the number of benefits applications coming in. Rather than continue pursuing a new scope of work, the state opted to hire a vendor to maintain what Nava had already built. The hope in working so closely with Vermont government staff had been that the state would continue to maintain the tools internally. But the new procurement indicated that the situation likely became untenable for existing government staff.

Because Nava's focus is on strategic projects that dramatically improve how vulnerable populations access government services, as opposed to purely maintenance and staff augmentation, they chose not to bid on the next portion of the work. As of this writing, the work is at a standstill.

"Phase three would have been launching this mobile-first, user-friendly, heavily user-tested online application to as many as 130,000 Vermonters, who typically call the call center," Fichera says. "That would have provided a lot of strategic value. But the pandemic took the wind out of the sails on that. Unfortunately, timing-wise, it overlapped with losing our internal champions. And the state fell back on the safe play."[55]

The technical contractor the state has used in the past is Optum, which built Vermont Health Connect for an estimated cost of $200 million and holds the maintenance contract.[56] In contrast, Nava's contracts have typically been capped at $500,000. As of this writing, whether Vermont uses Optum for the uploader maintenance contract remains to be seen.

Most of the people we interviewed about the project also pointed to another reason for the standstill: two of the project's biggest internal champions left the state. After nearly a decade in and around government, Cass Madison left in October 2019 to work on a public interest technology start-up. With Madison gone, Thani Boskailo found herself working with leadership who had not bought into the project's goals.

"The new project leadership had their own way of doing things and their own vision, which focused more on Big Bang approaches," Boskailo says.[57]

On top of that, remember those discussions around authentication, eligibility, and logging in that the Nava team had delayed in favor of launching an MVP? Unfortunately, it was now time for those conversations, with the project missing its primary champion. The initial excitement over the ease of uploading documents rather than mailing, faxing, or hand delivering had given way to an infinite loop of conversations around how people would log in and be authenticated. As with many government projects, authenticating users (making sure people are who they say they are) can be immensely complex. The Vermont team found themselves caught between multiple interpretations of federal authentication requirements and different layers of authentication requirements even within the state of Vermont. The Centers for Medicaid and Medicare Services (CMS)—the federal agency responsible for administering those health benefits—required that users authenticate themselves, but other agencies involved in the integrated benefits project countered that the state could not legally require that people authenticate themselves in order to apply online for benefits.

Boskailo compares her work life at that time to being a hamster on a wheel. As middle management, she felt squeezed between fighting for her team, trying to find middle ground with other Vermont benefits programs teams who would also be using the integrated benefits form, and leadership who didn't really understand why this couldn't just be a big bang project like all other IT projects. Shortly after Madison left, Boskailo followed suit.

Reflecting back on the experience, Boskailo thinks the integrated benefits project was missing an important change management piece. On the one hand, as much as Nava made sure to find internal champions, perhaps they didn't bring enough people with them on the journey. Embarking on an entirely new way of working is scary for anyone. For Vermont state employees up and down the chain, who had lived through the experience of hearing their efforts dragged through the mud every night on the local news during the launch of Vermont Health Connect, the prospect of doing all of that again—in the middle of a pandemic, no less—must have been terrifying.

On the other hand, Boskailo points out that anyone will buy into something that works. It's just a matter of proving that a careful, slower public interest technology approach works better for all involved than a massive big bang launch. Hopefully someday that time will come.

"I do miss the state of Vermont," Boskailo says wistfully. "I miss the work I did in serving Vermonters. One day, maybe I'll go back."[58]

In this chapter we've shared three stories to illustrate the three different elements involved in the practice of public interest technology. But it is important to note that even though we are calling out one specific element for each story, all the stories include an alchemy of design, data, and delivery work. No single element can stand on its own, and all three together are not an instant Easy Bake recipe for victory. But by using these three elements in combination you dramatically increase your likelihood of success.

All three stories also integrate technology in different ways, from a detailed technical build in the state of Vermont to Crisis

Text Line's algorithms and data mining. Civilla's work in Michigan only brushes by technology, yet it is a story that could only happen in the digital age. In the next chapter, we'll dig deeper on how technology factors into public interest technology, and also how it doesn't.

3

It's Not Just about Technology

NEARLY EVERYONE has been in that meeting. The one where someone proposes a new piece of technology to solve a problem. Homelessness or hunger or the racial gap in school achievement will be solved by an app, or by Blockchain, or a new database, or sensors, or machine learning, or maybe facial recognition. No matter the industry, the field, or the place, people love to propose a technological silver bullet. We have both seen this happen in multiple arenas. If you have read this far, you will understand that technology alone is never the antidote. Technology by itself won't end world hunger, and misused—as we will discuss later—it could make things worse.

When Hana was working with Transportation Safety Administration (TSA), the organization had barely gotten over the stinging public response to their randomizer app—a $50,000 app that randomly told passengers in security lines to go right or left, in an effort to reduce the public perception that TSA agents racially profile the people chosen for additional screenings. Despite the failure of the app, when confronted with a brand-new problem—security lines were too long, causing people to miss their flights and have to sleep overnight in the airport—TSA proposed solving the problem with . . . wait for it . . . an app. This new app was in addition to the cargo ship's worth of technology already being thrown at the problem of securely screening a public who doggedly insisted on packing full-sized toothpaste in their carry-ons.

Despite the fact that many of the people doing the work described in this book work for digital services or technology teams, nearly all of them strongly deemphasize the technology part of their work. Fixing intractable problems is never as simple as building an app. Todd Park puts it bluntly: "Tech is not a unilateral solution. Tech is not the point. The point is to actually improve outcomes."[1]

Everyone we interviewed for this book told us about understanding root problems, improving processes and culture, introducing service-oriented models, and changing the building blocks of how government solves problems. In fact, many public interest technology practitioners see technology as a way of getting a foot in the door to work on problems in a new way. That is, technology is a way of framing the problem that gets a better reception than offering to help with process or management.

Mikey Dickerson, the first administrator of USDS, found that if he walked into a meeting cold, he got a lot farther by saying he and his team were there to help with technology.

"Try saying you're going to the VA to be a management consultant. No. Don't bother," says Dickerson. "The technology label is a hack that works right now. Government's self-image is, there's this new technology bullshit that I don't understand because it's kids and their iPads and their Nintendos. In order to deal with that part, let's bring in some of those kids that understand the iPads and Nintendos."[2]

Vivian Graubard, also one of the founders of USDS, puts a finer point on it.

"In some ways, the technology angle was like a Trojan horse. Because every agency, every nonprofit wants to believe that a widget or an app is going to fix their problems. And if that's what gets us a seat at the table, then I'm okay with that being the lead-in and then having to work twice as hard to convince them otherwise. But at least I'm doing that from within the room versus trying to get them to see the world differently from step one."[3]

What these practitioners do not talk about is the new technology they implemented in their government agency. They may very well have implemented a cool new technology, but if they did it was in service of a larger purpose—speeding access to food security, breaking the cycle of poverty and incarceration, and so on—and therefore not the thing they are most proud of, nor the focus of their work. We call this work public interest technology because the approaches we emphasize—design, data, and delivery—are significantly affected by the evolving tools of the digital age. While technology itself can be an integral element, it is nearly always a combination of problem solving and management architecture, rather than a single technology itself, that drives transformation.

Staples, Not Software

The tools we describe in this book present a way in to see and solve a larger problem. But these methods often serve as an entry point to tackling larger problems in government. When Marina Nitze began working at the U.S. Department of Veterans Affairs as the chief technology officer (CTO), she used her tech and business process skills to win people's trust by solving a problem that was a pain for many of her coworkers.

A prodigious amount of work at the VA was done via paper folders, and she saw what a headache it was for her coworkers to keep track of who had which file folder, so she whipped up a simple program that allowed the agency to track the folders using bar codes. Even though Nitze had come to the agency with a larger plan around improving business processes (note that her ultimate goal was not a technical one, such as upgrading the mail server), she saw something she could do immediately to make people's lives easier.

"I wanted to automate how disability claims were processed, and I knew how to do that, I just didn't have resources or political buy in," she says. "Instead of going in day one announcing that was my plan, I just tried to be very quiet and listen and leverage the people that I had a relationship with, and ask them where I could be helpful to them. Whatever it was, I was willing to do that to help build the relationship."[4]

Because Nitze was a political appointee, her CTO role ended in 2016 as the Obama administration came to an end, and she began putting out the word that she'd like to work on foster care. She'd been around the foster care world since she was a college student with extra hours to spare.

"I like a varied amount of work and I like challenges, and this happened to be a varied amount of work and challenges that also gave back," Nitze told us.[5]

For the past fifteen years she has volunteered as a court-appointed special advocate for King County in Washington State, where her role is to be the eyes and ears of the court while ensuring that the state does the best it can to help children in the foster care system.

"I will help birth parents figure out how to get a bus pass. I will fill out the unbelievably large amount of paperwork to make sure that a sixth grader doesn't have to change schools the last two weeks of elementary school. I will help advocate that a child may need more or less mental health medication. And every six months I go to court for each child and recommend to the judge if parental rights should be terminated, or maybe the parents need additional services, or the child needs additional services," Nitze explains.[6]

The foster care arena is ripe for those seeking opportunities to help others. In America there are currently 400,000 children in foster care.[7] While coming into care may provide immediate protection from abuse and neglect, the long-term outlook is grim: 70 percent of juvenile justice–involved youth have been in the child welfare system,[8] 33 percent of homeless young adults were previously in foster care,[9] and 60 percent of youth who are sex trafficked were in care,[10] among many other sobering statistics. Across the country, hard-working, well-intentioned social workers are doing their best to help these kids, but they often lack the tools and resources to do their jobs and change the terrible outcomes of children in the system. In even well-funded counties, most work takes place on Post-It notes and IBM mainframes.

In 2017, a former boss of Nitze's had taken a cabinet position in Rhode Island working for the new governor, and knowing Nitze's interest in foster care he suggested she spend a few days in Rhode Island learning about the challenges their foster care system faced.

At that time, about two-thirds of the foster care kids in Rhode Island were going straight into group homes because there weren't enough beds for them with foster parents, even though the state's preference was to place children with families.[11] This made Rhode Island the fourth highest state in the nation in placing children into institutional or group settings. Rhode Island had decided that building a technical recruiting system would increase the number of beds in foster homes and solve the problem. But as Nitze started to dig into the issue, she quickly saw that the problem wasn't a lack of families who wanted to welcome foster children into their homes. In fact, the state had more applicants than they could handle. The problem was that getting families licensed was an onerous, time-consuming process.

Nitze recalls meeting with Adam Williams, a fellow with Foster America, an organization that places midcareer executives into high-level roles in child welfare. He had been working in Rhode Island and told her, "I'm recruiting [families], but then I have to hold their hand and personally jump through fifteen hurdles to get them through the licensing process because it's such a complicated process."[12]

After that conversation, Nitze began to see a solution take shape that had nothing to do with technology and nothing to do with recruiting. For most states, only 17 percent of applicants have obtained licenses a year and a half after they first apply, a dismal rate that calls into question why anyone would bother applying in the first place.

"It became clear to me that I didn't actually want to work on recruiting until I could help streamline licensing," Nitze explained. "Because the risk I saw was that you could recruit a bunch of families en masse, and if you didn't have Adam personally holding their hand and walking them through it, which is not a scalable resource, you could risk losing them forever."[13]

Recruiting families to apply for an arduous licensing process only to have them ultimately drop out was an exercise in futility. In fact, layering a technical solution to speed up recruitment on top of a broken process to get families licensed would have likely made things worse for Rhode Island, with more families stuck waiting for licenses and ultimately dropping out. Instead, Nitze kept her focus on the root problems rather than getting distracted by technology.

With a clear goal in mind—license families easier and faster—she conducted in-depth interviews to better understand why applicants dropped out of the process. What she learned was that, from the point of view of applicant families, a pervasive lack of trust in the department was eating away at the number of families who eventually got licensed. When they called to find out where they were in the process, what training classes were next, what paperwork was missing, no one answering the phone could tell them. Or they never got a call back.

"If you're treating me this way, when you're recruiting me, how are you going to treat me when I have a crisis in the middle of the night with an actual child?," Nitze says many families were likely wondering.[14]

Next, to better understand what was slowing the process down, Nitze spent time with Rhode Island's Department of Children, Youth and Families (DCYF), walking step by step through the process. Along with a software engineer and a researcher, the team visually mapped out the process in detail—a standard form of documentation for business process reengineering, but one that often does not take place in the public sector, where business processes have often evolved over centuries. Then they took the process map to Kinkos to have it printed out on huge sheets. The process was too long and convoluted to fit on a standard-size piece of paper. Kinkos printed the sheets for free when they learned that the project was to help foster children.

Once the process maps were printed up, the team took them around to unfurl in front of different individuals in the department to make sure they'd gotten it right. And then they began asking why. Why does it go this way when this way would be faster? Is this printed on blue paper because that's the law or because the person in charge likes blue? Is this point here really a legal requirement? Is it truly necessary?

In mapping out the process, one of many issues the team immediately identified that was not remotely tech-related involved giving the state consent to contact an applicant's doctor. The consent form was on a separate piece of paper from the main application, so applicants often forgot to submit it or erroneously sent it to their doctor, who usually didn't know what to do with it. The form also didn't have a place to put a doctor's phone number and address, which meant that when the child welfare department did receive the form, someone would have to pick up the phone and call the applicant to get the doctor's contact information.

The team's very high-tech innovation that solved this problem was . . . are you ready? A staple. They took the consent form and stapled it to the application, and the rate of failure for sending in the form went from 70 percent to zero.[15]

Another not remotely technical solution involved Social Security numbers. In mapping out the process the team discovered that the department never asked for Social Security numbers, because they believed, incorrectly, that asking people for their Social Security number was illegal. So the form didn't have a field for Social Security number. But part of the application process included running a background check. In order to run a background check on someone, you need that person's Social Security number. So families would submit their applications and then receive a voicemail from DCYF saying, "Hi, I need your Social Security number. Can you please call me back."

Nitze recalls, "People would very regularly tell us, 'That was the strangest phone call. I was definitely not calling you back. I thought it was Chinese spam or whatever.'"[16]

As a result, it took a very long time for the state to get the right information to run background checks. Sometimes background checks turn up things that automatically disqualify applicants, like an assault or a domestic violence conviction. Without the check, the department could end up wasting resources attempting to process applicants who were never going to make it through to become foster parents. The solution was to add a space for applicants to enter their Social Security numbers.

A Nontechnical Pilot

Meanwhile, Rhode Island had begun the process of procuring software to help them better manage foster care cases. As anyone familiar with the procurement process knows, purchasing the software was going to take time. Lots and lots and lots of time. But in reviewing the mapped-out process, Nitze saw that there were nontechnical changes that could speed the process up and begin working through the backlog of families waiting to get licensed. The more families who had licenses, the fewer kids who would be sent to group homes.

"I thought, okay, what are all the things we can do absent technology? And using Excel spreadsheets, a giant piece of butcher paper, and just a lot of elbow grease, we ran a pilot, called Recruitment Weekend," Nitze told us.[17]

Recruitment Weekend was a two-day event designed to clear the extensive backlog of families who had applied to be foster parents, while also validating in real time that a new, streamlined process would work. The team brought in onsite fingerprinting for background checks, had staff members ready to answer questions, and offered training classes so that families could finish the hours they needed over the course of one weekend. They even ran TB tests, offered fire extinguishers, and had a station where pets could be vaccinated and certified—all requirements for prospective families. The state invited all 300 families who had foster parent applications pending to the event. As a result of the weekend, 194 families received licenses. Prior to the weekend event there were only 174 families licensed to take children in the entire state. In one weekend, the team was able to double the supply of available families—all without writing a single line of code.

Another benefit of the weekend was that foster families got to know one another. Nitze says that the weekend helped build a community of foster parents, and gave them a positive experience to replace the tedious, negative experience of waiting a very long time to be approved. However, she cautions that foster care approval is not something that benefits from being too speedy.

"Do you want it to be like on Saturday morning I can decide I want to be a foster parent, and I do all my paperwork online, and it's instantly approved, and I sit and watch training videos and then Monday I'm ready to take a kid? I don't think that that's a healthy model that we want to have. People need time to think through it, they need different touch points with social workers, they need to really understand what are their expectations and what's realistic for the system."[18]

That said, families who make the decision to become foster parents certainly deserve an answer within a year and a half's time.

This is not to say that there isn't a role for technology in improving the foster care system overall. With the systems states currently have in place, it is difficult to search for available families in ways that mirror the real needs of children. Search tools often don't have school district boundaries that are updated for the current school year. Search is limited in the way that parameters overlap, which means that a search for a Spanish-speaking family in a specific elementary school might turn up zero results, when a Spanish-speaking family might live one district over. Nitze envisions a future system that never returns zero results—where there are always families available to take a child.

Technology is one tool that can help improve foster care if correctly applied. But it is not the only tool.

Tech Is a Tool, but It Is Rarely the Solution

Rhode Island is not unique in their foster care challenges. The federal government established today's child welfare IT requirements in 1993.[19] To put that in a technical context, Microsoft rolled out MS-DOS 6 the same year.[20] Those requirements touch many, many parts of the child welfare system, and the federal government provides funds for those elements. But licensing foster families is not one of them.

So just as every state has built their own system for federally funded programs like SNAP, every state has also had to develop their own foster care license tracking system. Many of these systems are on index cards or Post-It notes or Excel spreadsheets. With no federal funding, there was no money for a technological solution. So this is not to say that there isn't an obvious technical solution to the problem. But the majority of the work Nitze and her team have done is not technical—finding out where the problems are, what's holding up the process, and developing creative solutions. Those solutions included a group gathering, free fire extinguishers, and a staple, all working to fix the root problem: licensing was complex and slow.

In an excellent example of starting small, testing, and growing, Nitze has since expanded her work from Rhode Island to eight states and Washington, D.C., and as of this writing is working on an online playbook to capture best practices. One is to create a refrigerator magnet to help families track when they practice their fire evacuation plan (one of Michigan's requirements for licensing). Others include checklists, templates, and sample contract language. These are also not high-tech solutions. But they are what the foster care licensing process needs.

Anyone who has worked in or around government—or other large institutions—has come across a project conceived with the best of intentions, but undertaken as though technology is a magical wand that can dissolve bureaucracy, create internal processes where none exist, and repair broken workstreams. While Nitze's work on foster care is a success story, it is also an example of why public interest technology, despite the name, is not about fancy technology. It's not an approach that requires top-tier Silicon Valley talent, or access to drones, or a deep understanding of augmented reality. The story of foster care licensing in Rhode Island is the story of problem solving at its best, simplest, and most life-changing: the embodiment of the public interest technology mindset.

An app alone will never fix homelessness or end hunger. As we write, we have seen a bevy of calls for coronavirus hackathons, as though connecting a bunch of smart people who can write code could slow the transmission of a virus or magically develop a fully tested vaccine. Technology is a tool, an enabler, but rarely itself a solution.

"Sometimes it's fine to do things on paper," Nitze says. "The goal here is not to replace humans with robots and apps. Generally speaking, technology is an undercurrent, but there is so much you can get done with policy and practice changes. You just have to think about how you solidify the policy and practice changes that you need with the technology instead of the technology being the goal."[21]

Needs First, Then Technology

Even when technology turns out to be integral to a solution, it is never the first place to start. Technology was the last thing on Jos de Blok's mind when he first started thinking about how to improve nursing in the Netherlands. De Blok had loved working as a nurse. Back in the early days of his career, in the 1980s, he was responsible for a specific neighborhood in his native Holland (*buurt* in Dutch), and he had the opportunity to get to know individual patients. As was standard practice then, de Blok worked closely with his patients' physicians and social workers to create a holistic, carefully crafted treatment plan for each patient. But in the 1990s things changed.

The Dutch healthcare industry, heavily influenced by the U.S. system, began to look at healthcare as a range of products that could be bought and sold. In this model, doctors and nurses were effectively sellers of healthcare, patients were consumers, and market incentives dictated what services were available. What this meant in practice was that a profession that had previously relied on small local organizations now encompassed several regions, with multiple layers of management, and strategy teams, and resources departments.

Nurses who had previously enjoyed operating autonomously found themselves swimming in a sea of bureaucracy, dwarfed by bloated management structures. By this time de Blok had become the director of innovation at his organization, but he had eighteen work colleagues who were also directors of something. The layers of bureaucracy meant nurses spent most of their time filling out forms and handling administrative tasks rather than with patients. He watched as many of his fellow nurses became ill from the daily level of frustration or quit altogether.

De Blok thought about how to make a change to empower both nurses and patients, while still working within the existing regulations. Because he'd been a nurse and was surrounded by nursing colleagues, he knew the needs of nurses, so he didn't start with deep preliminary research into the world of nursing the way Marina Nitze and her team dove into foster care. Instead, de Blok's first step was to envision what the ideal healthcare world looked like from both the patient and nursing perspectives. What kind of organization would that look like?

He was also particularly concerned about the needs of terminally ill patients, who weren't going to get a second shot at their final healthcare experience. "If you are terminally ill and you're staying at home and you need support, it needs to be good because you can only do it once, this palliative, terminal phase."[22]

De Blok began putting together a plan for reinstituting community nursing, which would allow teams of nurses to care for designated neighborhoods. He talked over the idea with his friend Edwin Middendorp, who worked in tech at Facebook. Middendorp suggested building a tech backbone that would take care of all the mindless administrative tasks that nurses were currently mired in. Automating back office tasks would not only make life better for nurses and patients, it would also save money on staffing a back office. Instead, the money could be funneled into nursing.

Buurtzorg launched in 2006. Since then, the organization has grown to 15,000 people working in community nursing and teams of workers in domestic care, mental care, youth care, maternity care, and other areas. At its heart, Buurtzorg is made up of autonomous teams responsible for managing themselves and their patients' needs. When a new team is established, the team finds their own office space in the neighborhood they'll be serving. As though they are participating in an extended offsite team-building exercise, the team then organizes how they will work, who will be responsible for what, and how they will make decisions.

When the coronavirus came to the Netherlands, Buurtzorg's flexible structure meant that they organized themselves to procure personal protective equipment (PPE) for their nurses. While other healthcare organizations waited for the government to provide them PPE, Buurtzorg was set up to tackle the challenge themselves, purchasing one million masks from China, and making their own following guidance from Cuba and Taiwan.

But perhaps most surprising, given de Blok's focus on nurses and patients, is that a big part of Buurtzorg's success is the organization's proprietary technology that makes community nursing possible. Even though Buurtzorg did not start with technology, the tool they built is integral to how they are able to serve both patients and nurses. De Blok began by thinking about what nurses and patients really needed, what their days should look like—everything down to what office space would best support community nursing. Once all of the needs were defined, and only then, did his attention turn to how technology could support the ideal structure.

Over thirty home healthcare organizations now use the technology de Blok and Middendorp developed.[23] Since 2007, when the organization launched their first nursing team, Buurtzorg has grown to employ 8,000 nurses in 700 teams, across twenty-four countries. An Ernst and Young study found that if Buurtzorg's model were universally implemented throughout the Netherlands, the healthcare system would save 40 percent of its current expenditures. De Blok also met his initial goal of providing better care to patients and a better working environment for nurses. Government surveys show Buurtzorg's patients to be highly satisfied with their care, and Buurtzorg's employees rank as the most satisfied workforce of any Dutch company with more than 1,000 employees.[24]

––––––

The lure of starting with technology, or technology as panacea, can be hard to overcome. Governments are often inundated with vendors looking to apply machine learning or predictive analytics to solve problems. We have encountered many agencies over time who have succumbed to the siren song of the flashiest, sexiest, sleekest new thing. Police departments, for example, often own the latest and greatest weapons, while lacking an easy way to capture arrest data.

The key is to regard technology as one of the many tools in a problem solver's tool kit. That tool kit is rich with information just waiting to be unlocked—untapped data waiting to be thoughtfully analyzed, end users eager to tell their stories. But technology only helps if you have a clear understanding of the problem you are trying to solve.

Todd Park, former White House CTO, recounts that in his experience working with federal agencies, the means and the ends were frequently conflated. Often USDS would go to an agency and ask, "What are you trying to accomplish with this project?" And agency staffers would reply, "I'm trying to accomplish the building of the software." Park says the USDS team would then push to help people see beyond the technology.

"Oh, is it actually to dramatically improve the efficiency and speed and user experience of immigrating to America? Okay. If that's the goal, then we can help you leverage technology to get to that goal."[25]

In the work of Nitze and de Blok we see evidence of both the emergence and the impact of public interest technology. Both put users at the center of their work, used real-time data to guide their thinking, and started small and tested out strategies before scaling.

If you use the tools we are laying out in this book, you will likely find, as those we profile did, a way to use technology to help find or improve the right policy solution. But remember that the technology is only as good as the design process, which starts and ends with the interests of the people a program intends to serve. As we will explain in the next chapter, technology can be used to understand which policy solutions are needed and to help make those solutions work for people. But technology cannot replace good policy design.

4

User-Centered
Policy Design

ROCKFORD, ILLINOIS, a small city on the Rock River halfway between Chicago and the Iowa border, has seen a lot of innovations come and go over the years. The town's main industry has morphed from fine furniture making in the 1800s to the production of immense heavy machinery up through the 1980s, when that industry shrank and then left town.[1] The aerospace industry moved in, but remnants of the manufacturing boom still dot the town in the form of abandoned factories. The art deco Coronado Theater—listed on the National Registry of Historic Places—embodies the dreams of past Rockfordians, while down the block empty storefronts speak to present realities. Before coronavirus hit the United States, the town's unemployment rate was higher than the national average, and at the time of this writing, Rockford's unemployment rates were more than 20 percent.[2]

Like many towns of former glory, Rockford has always had a persistent homeless population. As a policy challenge, homelessness frustrates local leaders around the world. But in 2015 Rockford ended veterans' homelessness. In 2017 they ended chronic homelessness, and as of this writing are on track to do the impossible: end homelessness entirely.[3] The city's experience has lessons for policy design at all levels of government. In this chapter we will examine those lessons and contrast them with something very different, the way in which Congress has approached economic relief during the pandemic.[4]

Really Understanding the Problem

Addressing and serving the homeless population is usually done by a fragmented coalition of actors and organizations in a community or city, each touching the lives of a homeless person with a different service or interaction. Hospitals serve their health needs. Shelters and housing support agencies provide beds in shelters. Police keep records of who has been cited for loitering. Every nonprofit and agency collects data on their part of the work, but there is no comprehensive list that provides a snapshot of the individuals who are experiencing homelessness.

The team that succeeded in ending homelessness in Rockford started with a simple idea: know who you are trying to house. The team was part of a larger movement of teams all using the same methodology across the nation to combat homelessness, called Built for Zero. Rockford's Built for Zero team began with homeless veterans, who made up a significant population of the city's homeless. While there were many organizations in Rockford that touched veteran homelessness, there was no single entity responsible for the entire community. The team began by making a list of every single veteran in Rockford who was homeless, so they could understand the totality of Rockford's homeless population and their needs. But the list creation process also did something else. It changed the problem being solved from a series of disconnected inputs—number of beds filled, number of people fed, number of patients served— to a concrete and shared goal that centered on human lives.

Ultimately, the list changed the focus from numbers of beds and meals and services to one single number: people who remain homeless.

"Every veteran has a name. Every person has a story," says Larry Morrissey, the former mayor of Rockford. "When we make their story part of our story and our life and our work, we're able to get people housed, we're able to manage that list, and we're able to make the connections to solve that problem."[5]

By working down the list, Built for Zero and the team in Rockford were able to make policy recommendations that got to the root causes of Rockford's homeless population. Those recommendations grew from suggestions to pilots to functioning city policy.

But this isn't normally how policy is designed.

Educated Guessing: The Standard Policy Design Process

Imagine that a friend calls you with an urgent task. They know of a family who needs your help. Now. The family is down to their last meal with no idea where the funds for their next one will come from. Your friend asks if you could shop for groceries at the market and drop them off. This shopping trip is urgent, your friend stresses. Without your help the family might starve. Your friend goes into great detail about how to pay for the groceries—you are to use three $20 bills and one $50—then hangs up. As you are headed to the market you realize you are missing a few necessary pieces of information. Your friend didn't tell you how many family members there are or any information about where the family lives. You don't know if the family has a functional refrigerator or if their electricity has been shut off. You have no idea if they have food allergies, how old their kids are, or if they have older family members with specific dietary needs. What would you do?

Most likely, you would make an educated guess.

This is how Cecilia Muñoz, former Domestic Policy Council director under President Obama, characterizes the current method of policy design. Muñoz is a self-described "policy nerd." In the White House, she served eight years under President Obama, where she oversaw policy decisions on areas including public health, education, immigration, and criminal justice. Before moving to the White House, Muñoz spent decades as the policy director for the largest Hispanic civil rights organization in the United States. If anyone knows the policy making process, it is Muñoz. But as she reflects back on her more than three decades of work on policy, she can see that the toolbox needs improvement: "At best it is really good educated guessing. All the wonderful, well-meaning people, including me [in my former positions] are kind of flying blind."[6]

As an example of the vagaries of the policy process, Muñoz shared her experience on White House criminal justice work. When it came to reducing recidivism—helping to shrink the number of formerly incarcerated people who return to jail— there was no available data on what worked, she says, even for the nation's most senior advisors and experts.

"Six hundred thousand people leave incarceration each year. We don't even collect data on what happens to them [when they leave prison]. None," Muñoz says.[7]

The lack of data means that the only way experts can make policy recommendations on reducing recidivism is guesswork. This lack of data isn't a mistake or an oversight. It's the norm.

Muñoz is not the only one who describes policy design in this way. Tom Loosemore, cofounder of the UK's Government Digital Service and coauthor of an excellent book of advice for

those starting a digital government team,[8] uses strikingly similar language to describe policy making, calling it "educated
guesswork" and "a feedback loop measured in years."[9]

When government and policy makers do collect data, it is
usually through studies that are designed to learn if a program
worked, often conducted by separate scholars, years later. There
is often no system for monitoring, in real-time, the experience
of those impacted by a policy. When such a tool exists, it is
often not designed to deliver the data in a way that makes it usable to those overseeing policy.

In California, for example, the delivery of unemployment
insurance is broken into different departments, with one team
overseeing the call center and another overseeing the website.
Each team sees the data that relates to their piece of work. Like
the parable of blind men each describing an elephant based on
the small piece of the animal they are touching, seeing only one
small part of customer data makes it impossible to paint a picture of the totality of the customer experience.

Public policy making and public administration use economic analysis and statistics to size up problems and calculate
the impact a given policy will have once it is running at full
scale. These tools are important. They are useful in determining
the cost of a policy or the correlation between interventions
and outcomes, or in developing scenarios for how a given policy might reach specific populations. Economists and statisti-
cians are pretty good at answering questions like *How much will
it cost the government to pay for this?* or *How many families could
be eligible?* But the current tools are not particularly useful for
understanding the needs of a population, nor are they helpful
in assessing in real time whether a policy is working the way it
was intended. To collect this information, someone who is
tech-fluent must be present at the policy table.

"Every major policy issue, when it's being decided, there's a lawyer in the room and there's an economist in the room. There now needs to be a public interest tech person in the room," says Todd Park. "It doesn't necessarily need to be someone who is a literal engineer or a UX [user experience] person or product manager. But it should be someone who's deeply versed in what tech is capable of doing and, equally importantly, what it cannot do."[10]

Most of the fastest-growing companies today are powered in part by the real-time assessment of what people are using and what they are interested in. These companies are populated by product managers, user researchers, and data analysts who work together to ensure that all pieces of the end product adequately meet both the goals of the company and users' goals. But these tools and roles haven't yet been incorporated widely into how government makes policy and monitors the results. Not only should these skills and mindsets be present in the building of systems, but they must also be incorporated into an agency's core mission and decision-making machinery. While the tools of economics and statistics are crucial, we need to expand the inputs we use for both policy design and delivery.

To understand why the current approach to policy doesn't work, let's look at a recent high-stakes policy process that affected a significant percentage of the U.S. population: one of the early coronavirus-related economic stimulus packages.

What It Looks Like to Ignore Design, Data, and Delivery

By the beginning of March 2020 the bottom was falling out of the economy. As Americans sheltered in place to reduce the spread of COVID-19, unemployment skyrocketed and economic activity plummeted. Politicians and economists agreed something had to be done to address the economic fallout. Even Republicans, many of whom came to power as part of a backlash against government spending during the Great Recession, were feeling the need to act.

Senate Majority Leader Mitch McConnell gave the holdouts in his party advice on how to mix their orthodoxy on spending with the urgency of the moment. "My counsel to them is to gag and vote for it anyway, even if they think it has some shortcomings."[11]

In March 2020, Congress passed the Coronavirus Aid, Relief, and Economic Security Act, also known as the CARES Act, a massive, 880-page[12] economic stimulus, more than double the stimulus act passed in 2009 during the financial crisis. The bill came together the way bills usually do in a crisis—rapidly, with experts weighing in but little or no information directly from average Americans, and with no piloting or testing.

Businesses lobbied congressional offices for aid, and state and local governments put in their requests as well. Boeing, the aerospace giant, asked for $60 billion. The airline industry petitioned for another $50 billion in aid. The U.S. Conference of Mayors, an association of city mayors, sent a letter appealing for $250 billion in aid to cities.[13] Industries from tourism and travel to alcohol and beverages aggressively lobbied Congress. Much of this lobbying worked. Boeing and the airline industry won huge financial relief. The Distilled Spirits Council, the lobbying arm for America's alcohol producers, received a tax break to help distilleries switch from making alcohol to producing hand sanitizer. Some lobbying shops, like the K Street firm Holland & Knight, even set up a "Covid-19 Response Team."[14]

Policy experts from think tanks played their role in the policy creation process as well, writing memos and publishing papers on what Congress should do. Experts inside and outside of government weighed in with memos full of analysis about what worked in past recessions and what didn't.

There are two different starting points on the size of investment necessary to resuscitate the economy, based on where lawmakers fall on the political spectrum. One party sees workers, state governments, and small business as the engine; the other sees support to large businesses as critical. Using these starting points, bolstered by the lobbying, memo writing, and expertise offered, party leaders outlined policy proposals over the course of three weeks.

But while business associations have full-time lobbyists to give voice to their needs, and think tanks represent different political leanings or niche issues, there aren't many influential associations representing most people. *Politico* reporter Michael Grunwald described the back-and-forth for the CARES Act as "an inside game." When asked to describe who really drives the content of what's in and what out of a bill, he described it as a "remarkably small circle."[15]

The act was hashed out and amended in ways that seem abstract and occasionally border on capricious. The first version of the bill aides presented to President Trump was for an $850 billion package. He is reported to have asked, "Why not make it a trillion?" Lawmakers quickly obliged. Over the following weeks the size of the package doubled again in an effort to appease both Democratic requests for aid to the states and Republican support for businesses. More cash for families also went in—a policy that had bipartisan support.

Grunwald, a frequent chronicler of economic stimulus packages, summed up the process as "not exactly the triumph of democracy."

This legislative sausage making, brought to life for most Americans in the eighty-plus-year-old film *Mr. Smith Goes to Washington*, has looked the same for generations.[16]

Here's what wasn't part of the process: a rapid review of what would help the average family suffering economically from COVID-19. While the Distilled Spirits Council and the airline industry have mechanisms for immediately understanding what their member companies need, there is no similar feedback loop for most Americans, especially those who are the most vulnerable. The process for surveying what people need is normally done through hearings or committees—experts are invited to share their perspectives with elected officials. Because the CARES bill moved fast, there wasn't time for this part of the process. But even so, expert testimony is no replacement for listening to the real voices of the public, especially because those who have the most at stake often have no voice. And the ways the public used to be heard no longer work that well. There were vociferous calls from unions like the Service Employees International Union (SEIU) to Congress to focus on the needs of working people, but today only 11 percent of American workers are represented by a union.[17]

In the rush to release funds, the tools espoused in this book—human-centered design research, real-time data instrumentation, and testing big ideas in a small way before rolling them out—were not deployed, and it shows. We are not suggesting that Congress should have paused at this very moment to implement these tools. Moving fast in a crisis is critical. The larger issue is that there is no way currently for Congress to rapidly conduct user research, monitor real-time data, or run a pilot, and therefore lawmakers' mindsets are not guided by public interest technology thinking.

The law allocated $300 billion for one-time coronavirus relief payments to most American adults, but very little thought went into how these dollars would reach people. For example, fourteen million American adults have no bank accounts.[18] You don't need to do a user survey to know that some of the most vulnerable Americans will be hard to reach through a system focused on direct deposit payments. So it is not surprising that within the first month, less than half of the people the law intended to help with emergency cash relief received payments. These intended recipients faced looming rent payments, overdue bills, or car payments with no income and no federal help. For many Americans the payments weren't just a nice-to-have cushion. They meant survival.

In order to get a stimulus check from the federal government, an applicant must have filed a tax return previously. But ten million low-income families don't earn enough to file taxes.[19] It took weeks and a national outcry for the IRS to build out a site for nonfilers. Unfortunately, the form also required an e-mail address, which not everyone has, particularly those who might already be on society's fringes and most in need of help. Without a COVID Response lobbying team, those ten million people's needs weren't addressed in ways that could actually help them.

Even the people who regularly file tax returns weren't necessarily covered. The physical delivery methods for transferring cash had also not been thought through as a part of the bill. Since 100 million taxpayers don't have direct deposit information on file with the IRS, that meant that they wouldn't see any money until checks could get printed and mailed, which could take months.[20] People trying to log into the IRS portal to find out where their checks were received "status not available" messages for days. Six months after the CARES Act was passed, the IRS sent nine million people a letter suggesting that they were eligible for a stimulus check but still needed to act to receive it.[21]

It also wasn't clear that the size of payments was correct. Individuals were allocated $1,200 and families $2,400, regardless of income tax bracket. This meant that a family of four making $25,000 a year and a family of four making $150,000 a year received the same size check. Organizations quickly sprang up to help fix the discrepancy—people who had received checks they didn't need could donate their stimulus dollars to those who did—suggesting that the government erroneously helped those who didn't need help while ignoring those who did.[22] Had Congress reached out to speak with families and individuals in different tax brackets, or leaned on experts who had done so, lawmakers would have rapidly understood which families would really be helped by the payout and which families might be fine without it.

This wasn't the only part of the CARES Act to run into delivery problems. The Payroll Protection Program (PPP), a part of the bill aimed at helping small businesses, ran out of money twelve days after it launched, necessitating the creation of a second bill to help fill the meteor-sized holes in the first one. But the funds moved quickly to small and large companies—the ones who had been vocal about their needs and who already had established pathways for exchanging money with the government.

Numerous reports surfaced of businesses that couldn't even remotely qualify as a small business receiving money through CARES, among them fast-food chain Shake Shack, high-end restaurant chain Ruth's Chris Steak House,[23] and even the Los Angeles Lakers, a $4.4 billion franchise. But for true small businesses, the help was very uneven. At the same time, many of the people suffering the most found the requirements in the bill meant that they didn't qualify for help.

For several years, Margaret Coleman had run the T. W. Wood Gallery, an arts nonprofit in Montpelier, Vermont. The gallery earned its revenue from after-school art programs and donations. Those two sources evaporated as a result of school closures and the economic downturn. She had to lay off her entire staff. Coleman cut her own hours down to ten a week, which she spent exclusively applying for grants. The amount her organization needed to make it through the pandemic shutdown months was about $10,000, but there was nowhere to get that amount of money.

"Compared to other organizations, that amount is minimal," she said. "But it's not there."[24]

Her nonprofit should have been eligible for $18,000 through the PPP, but because that money could only be applied to payroll, she would have had to rehire the employees she laid off, at a rate several hundred dollars less than they were able to earn through unemployment insurance. Instead she hired new people at $16 an hour for the two-month period covered by PPP, fully expecting that in two months the economy would still be in tatters, schools would still be closed, and the money from CARES would be gone.

Efforts to expand unemployment benefits were also stymied by failure. The bill added $260 billion of unemployment insurance benefits, which meant that more people were eligible for unemployment than ever before in our nation's history. The statewide unemployment systems, already on the brink of collapse due to decades of neglect, promptly crashed under the tsunami of filers unleashed by the CARES Act, leaving people uncertain as to how to get the funds they knew they'd been promised.[25] While the CARES Act did provide much needed relief to the economy and millions of families, it fell short when it came to *how* these benefits reached those families.

Economic Coronavirus Relief That Worked

Coronavirus has touched nearly every nation on Earth; the varying ways governments dealt with the same situation offer interesting points of comparison. In Berlin, Germany, just five days after the application for financial relief became available, more than $1.4 billion had reached freelancers like writers and artists, fashion designers, computer programmers, hair stylists, web designers, and small shop owners. Germany's interventions at the city and national level received attention for both their scale[26] and delivery.

Wolfgang Schmidt, the state secretary of Germany's Ministry of Finance, said that the team working on getting relief payments out to Germans knew that speed was essential. Not only did the team rely on existing pipelines they knew would work to get the payments out, but they also drastically reduced the number of forms people were required to fill out and eliminated means testing—a calculation that normally dictates who is eligible for funds, and for how much.

"We can't do something that might be a good idea but would only be delivered two or three or four months later. When we thought about what to do and how to deliver it we said, 'Okay, let's rely on existing structures—if we want to deliver a quick result then we can't do means testing, and we can't do a lot of paperwork. Let's keep the application form simple and let's be generous. Yes, you will have people who are not entitled, we're going to figure that out later.'"[27]

In part informed by their experience handling the 2008 recession, and their more recent refugee crisis, the German government moved at breakneck speed. The cabinet met on a Monday to craft the policy, and by Friday both the senate and the parliament had adopted the measures. The federal president signed them into law that Saturday.

"I've been in politics for twenty years now. I've never seen something like that," Schmidt says.[28]

Several other countries also put together rapid economic relief. In Denmark, ten different parties in Parliament came together to pass a stimulus package that included paying private companies 75 percent of their payroll if they kept workers employed.[29] The Netherlands, too, passed a relief bill in March 2020 that made it easier for companies to recoup lost revenue and pay employees, and provided self-employed residents who earned less than minimum wage with government relief. The bill had no spending cap.[30]

Obviously, politics factors greatly into pieces of this story. The decision not to include a spending cap in the Netherlands, or to take German citizens at their word when they applied for funds, while also speeding delivery, is inextricably intertwined with those nations' alignment with the politics of social democracy and the role of the welfare state. The decision to prioritize corporate voices in the United States' CARES Act was political too.

But Germany's success wasn't only about the *what* of an economic recovery package; it was deeply about the *how*. The German government was responsive to both politics and process. Those with strong differences of opinion put party bickering aside to work quickly. Leaders also focused on the lived experience of those in need and made policy adaptations such as waiving means testing in order to be responsive to what they knew citizens really needed. Delivery won't fix bad policy, but very good policy can be undercut if it isn't designed and executed to meet people where they are.

Putting People First in Policy Design

So what should the policy design process look like? Let's go back to Rockford, Illinois, and their list of homeless veterans.

The list idea actually originated not in Rockford, but halfway across the country in Times Square, New York City. In 2003, Common Ground, a nonprofit dedicated to ending homelessness, and the organization that gave birth to the Built for Zero initiative, was working to house the significant homeless population who called the twenty-block area around Times Square home. The team had created permanent housing by renovating old, run-down hotels—restoring the structures to their original grandeur—and locating social workers and health services in the buildings. But once a person had been identified as a candidate for free or low-cost housing, the organization found itself mired in arduous bureaucratic hurdles to get people housed. They also found that the least vulnerable people were able to navigate the system, but the most needy couldn't, and as a result did not end up housed in their buildings. Every day Common Ground staff passed dozens of homeless en route to work. They were confronted on a daily basis by the personification of their failure.

The Common Ground CEO, Rosanne Haggerty, suggested that the team take a different approach. Instead of sitting at their desks coming up with solutions, Haggerty wanted her staff to leave the building and ask the homeless in the area what it would take to get them into housing. To spearhead this effort, she hired Army Intelligence officer and West Point graduate Becky Margiotta as the director of the Street to Home Initiative. Margiotta had experience learning about people's lives and motivations quickly, which she brought to her work at Common Ground. The team switched their hours from regular 9 a.m. to 5 p.m. business hours to 10 p.m. to 7 a.m. so that they could be present when they were needed most. Margiotta and her team were patient. Sometimes they sat silently with people in the area, saying nothing, but slowly building trust. Over time, they were able to identify every unhoused person in the vicinity of Times Square. They developed an approximate count and came to know people by name. Finally, after gaining a deep understanding of the people they were aiming to serve, the team worked case by case to get people housed.

On a weekly basis, Common Ground pulled together the relevant agencies and worked through their list of unhoused people. For each person, a team member would hold up their file and ask, "Who has seen this person this week?" Then, together, the team would identify the roadblocks for moving that person into housing. For example: *The last thing this person needs before he can apply for housing is a TB test. If he shows up at any of our doors, let's all agree we'll send him to Steve over at the clinic. Steve, will you be ready to fast-track him?*

This process forced all players involved to personally navigate a deeply complex, nearly labyrinthine system, leading them to a single truth: the system didn't help the people it was meant to serve. When the team reworked the structure with a focus on people and how they fared through the morass of rules, the results were impressive. There was an 87 percent reduction in homelessness in Times Square.

After their success in Times Square, Community Solutions received requests from other communities. The team figured that if their method worked on the congested streets of New York City, it might work elsewhere. So they began to scale their approach, with a nationwide campaign to house 100,000 chronically homeless, an effort that eventually became Built for Zero. Today Built for Zero is a network of dozens of communities willing to commit to reaching zero with some portion of their homeless population. The first community to meet their goal was Rockford.

Get the Right People in the Room

The Rockford Built for Zero team consisted of many organizations working as one. At the center of this action were three people: Angie Walker and Jennifer Jaeger of the city's Human Services Department, and Larry Morrissey, the mayor of Rockford.

Morrissey grew up in the community and describes himself as a "recovering lawyer" who likes to sink his teeth into policy. Beyond his interest in challenging problems, Morrissey had personal reasons guiding his focus on the homeless. His father was a veteran who had struggled for years with alcoholism.

"When I was a kid growing up, I would ask my father, 'Dad, why do you always give money out to people on the street?'" Morrissey recounts. "And he said, 'But for the grace of God, that could have been me.'"[31]

When a 2014 challenge from President Obama called on cities to end veteran homelessness, that call to action, combined with Morrissey's personal interest, led Rockford to start with the homeless veteran population. Along with seventy-six other mayors across the country,[32] Morrissey committed Rockford to the zero goal, but privately he was uncertain how the city would reach it. He was intent on addressing homelessness, but after several efforts didn't pan out he had grown cynical and reluctant to make a promise he couldn't keep. Ultimately, however, he took the pledge to end veteran homelessness, not knowing exactly how he would get it done, but hopeful that a solution was out there.

Along with the challenge, the Obama administration provided training and resources through the Department of Housing and Urban Development (HUD). In the winter of 2015, Morrissey, Walker, and Jaeger all traveled to Chicago for the training. They went in not knowing what to expect from the training, but Morrissey says it was a turning point. Experts from HUD broke down the methods and approaches that were working to reduce homelessness nationally. They featured cases from cities that were making progress, like New Orleans. The training also emphasized the use of data and the unified list concept that had been developed and tested in the 100,000

Homes campaign. Leaving the training, Morrissey thought, "We can do this."

When Morrissey returned from the training, he worked with Rockford's Built for Zero team to pull the all-important list together. Local hospitals, shelter providers, and others working with the homeless collected and shared data, which they aren't typically set up to do, all in service of the list-making process. Built for Zero worked with local leaders to create data sharing guidelines that would work across these varying institutions.

Rockford started with simple Google tools and iterated on designs based on monthly feedback. They collaboratively tracked their progress through dashboards and data visualizations. The list-making process also brought three disparate teams together for monthly meetings. Typically, government meetings include only one level of bureaucratic hierarchy. But in Rockford, the mayor and agency leadership, city nonprofits, and a tactical field team began meeting once a month to assess progress on the list, review operations, and work through issues.

Elsewhere, technology often takes the place of these kinds of meetings. Social service agencies are required to comply with federal regulations requiring the collection of data through Homelessness Management Information Systems (HMIS). These federally driven data management systems are paid for by communities to aid in reporting data points to Congress in order to receive federal homelessness grant dollars.

But the team in Rockford flipped the approach on its head. They set aside federal data compliance and focused on the data they would need to reduce homelessness in Rockford. They found that simply getting people in the same room once a month worked a lot better than the $33,764 they spent in 2012 on a federally mandated data system.

Once Rockford had a list of all local homeless veterans—about 100—the city was able to work down the list to get it to zero. Having a number to focus on pulls a problem out of fuzzy abstraction into concrete reality. *Ending veteran homelessness feels like a big job. Helping these 100 people find housing* feels more contained, and more human.

"When you talk about an actual human being, who's got a name, one you can find living under a bridge, and you could put his name on a board, then assemble a team that could develop a custom solution for that individual, that was really the difference maker," Morrissey says.[33]

The city also shared the numbers with the public at their RockStat meetings, where city statistics were regularly announced and updated, bringing public accountability and a spotlight to the project.

When Data Gives the What, Research Will Reveal the Why

After assembling the list, the team in Rockford began to dig into the underlying reasons behind homelessness in the veteran population. They soon unearthed one surprising cause: *bus fare.* If veterans have mental health issues, and transportation costs are out of their reach, they miss provider appointments, can't renew needed medications, and quickly find themselves fighting addiction and out on the street. In their conversations with veterans, the team heard multiple variations of this story over and over again. They learned that many vets needed help with transportation to doctor's appointments and other essential visits. That is, a significant underlying cause for veteran homelessness in Rockford came down to bus fare. This is the kind of nuanced finding that appears when teams dig to find the root cause of a problem. Imagine what this kind of work might have led to in developing the CARES Act.

Rockford city leaders saw in the bus fare finding that there was potentially a simple policy solution to help keep veterans from becoming homeless: free bus passes. As an experiment, they handed out sixty free temporary bus passes to veterans. The experiment successfully contributed to a drop in veteran homelessness. Rockford and its surrounding county now permanently offer discounted transportation for veterans.

Using Data, Design, and Delivery to Shape Policy

The list maintenance and regular data gathering also provided an essential on-ramp to understanding the root causes that led Rockfordians to become homeless. Once the team assembled their list and, over the course of a year, monitored the data monthly, they saw that the population of newly homeless was increasing. Even if they housed every person on their list, there was a steady inflow of new people. This insight led the team to understand that a potential solution would be to prevent homelessness before it started. So that is what the team decided to work on next.

In Rockford, landlords are required to give a five-day warning before they get a court order for their tenants to leave. As part of work to end family homelessness, the team reached out to landlords as soon as the five-day notice went out. They brought in mediators, offered to cover part of the rent, or worked to put vulnerable tenants on a payment plan. They also helped connect families to other services—child care or medical care—that could help them stay in their homes.

Leaders in Rockford could have attempted to solve veteran homelessness and chronic homelessness in their city by using standard policy practices. They could have passed legislation providing more funds for shelters, or criminalizing loitering. But instead they started with data and user research. They tried out different approaches and monitored their impact. They learned that ending homelessness meant first fixing adjacent problems such as slowing evictions and making transportation more affordable.

Standard policy meant to reduce homelessness usually relies on increasing funding for shelters or criminalizing loitering. Discounted transportation and eviction mediation are not normally part of the homelessness policy tool kit. But once the Rockford team began to ask the right questions, those elements became part of the obvious policy solution. Within the Built for Zero network, eighty-two cities and counties across the country are using similar methods to end homelessness. Of those, twelve have ended chronic or veteran homelessness. Barring a dramatic shift, if all eighty-two succeed, the organization could potentially reduce the number of homeless Americans by 20 percent. Since 2015, more than 120,000 people have been housed thanks to these efforts.

After their success ending veteran homelessness, the Rockford team moved on to end chronic homelessness and then to completely eliminate homelessness in their city. After five years, they succeeded. The chronic homeless population as of this writing amounts to two, and the team is poised to meet their goal of ending homelessness completely.

So why did we tell you this story? Eliminating homelessness in one midsized town in Illinois may seem like an entirely different problem than preventing pandemic-related economic fallout on a national scale. But consider that in 2020, Congress spent $2.8 billion on programs to address homelessness. Congress also spends $7 million on HMIS data systems annually,[34] most of which goes to six vendors. While HMIS vendors have adapted to create by-name lists, they largely remain focused on HUD compliance rather than community-driven demands for data tools that solve their problems. HUD also spends significant resources on a point-in-time data count every year that leaders on the ground describe as having minimum value in part because the point-in-time count is self-reported.

Despite these investments, nationally a steady 1 percent of Americans remain homeless.[35] While in many cases lack of funding appears to present an issue, Rockford had the dollars they needed. What they were lacking was insight into the underlying problems and the initiative to work together across agencies and organizations to solve them. Once they could see who they were serving and what their challenges were, they were able to develop and test workable solutions.

As of this writing, the number of homeless across the United States is skyrocketing, with tent encampments occupying city parks in towns like Springfield, Illinois,[36] and Wheeling, West Virginia.[37] This pandemic-related homelessness is different at its root than the type of homelessness that Built for Zero has worked on, and will likely require different policy interventions. But the only way to know is to do the work.

Why Policy Makers Need to Care about Policy Implementation

Historically, the work of implementing policy is often siloed away from policy making. Some people come up with the big ideas; another set of people bring them to market. Very few people in nonprofits and governments have the mandate that was given to Community Solutions staff to get out of the building and ask the people at the center of the problem what it would take to fix it. Historically, implementation has been the work of technocrats who do the sweat labor of bringing benefits or tax credits to the public.

Graduate school programs from public administration to public policy should be the grounds for training our public sector leaders in modern, real-world techniques, but they too fall short. Francis Fukuyama, professor of public policy and former senior State Department leader, puts it bluntly: "Most programs train students to become capable policy analysts, but with no understanding of how to implement those policies in the real world."[38]

This is outdated nineteenth- or twentieth-century thinking. Problem solving in the twenty-first century must be more iterative, data-driven, and hands-on. Jake Maguire of Community Solutions calls this "adaptive problem solving."[39] Accordingly, proposed solutions must include a feedback loop with the public that is shorter than years and decades. Problem solvers must have the space to test, learn, and improve. The experiences of the pioneers profiled in this book demonstrate that getting close to the people you are serving, improving monitoring capacity, and thinking through the details around how your policy reaches people have policy implications. In order to ensure that policy makers are putting the right policy in place, they must first understand the problems lying beneath the particular problem their policy is aimed at solving.

The lessons learned about homelessness in Rockford and the other eighty-one Built for Zero communities should inform state and federal homeless policy design. But for that to happen, the walls between policy design and policy implementation must come down. Some experts we interviewed suggested that the system needs to be turned on its head and become responsive to policy implementers, not just policy makers. Several prominent graduate schools of public policy have begun this work by offering classes that make clear the interlocking nature of policy design and implementation. The Policy Innovation Lab at Carnegie Mellon, for example, gives policy students the opportunity to work on real-world policy challenges using a public interest technology approach that includes designing with user research, testing and iterating on solutions, and ultimately informing policy design via implementation.[40]

Cecilia Muñoz, the veteran policy maker, gets animated talking about the opportunity that lies ahead for the next generation of policy makers to get closer to what is happening to families.

"I want to take people by the lapels to policy makers who want to get it right, get dollars in families' pockets, and erase disparity. Our standard operations miss and fail to reach those who need help the most. These tools exist in other spheres. You need to know how to use them," Muñoz says. "You are using a hammer and chisel in the digital age. You don't have to."[41]

Here's what that looks like in practice:

If you are a tax policy expert, you need to get curious about why 20 percent of the eligible public leaves the Earned Income Tax Credit (EITC) unclaimed. The EITC is one of the most effective vehicles for bringing families out of poverty,[42] but it's only effective if people use it. States are currently working across the country to expand the benefit, but for working families who would like to use it, accessing the credit is still so complicated that $1.4 billion annually is left unclaimed. Policy makers working on this issue haven't solved the problem if they have developed a solution that 1.2 million households can't use.

If you are a congressional staffer drafting the next stimulus package for people in need, you might be focused on how to get your drafted legislation out of committee and onto the floor.

But before you sign off on legislation, map out how your law actually gets to the public. Which agency must act to create regulations? How will funds get from the Treasury into people's wallets? How will people who need this service learn about it? You want to be careful that your law hasn't ordered up the impossible. Call someone who will be on the front lines of an agency or nonprofit delivering this to the public and ask what they think about the solution you've developed. Then call a family who might benefit and see if your proposal will actually help. Do that a few times over. You may be surprised by what you discover.

If you are an agency leader, you must understand that your biggest policy achievements rely entirely on your agency's ability to deliver them to the public. Make sure you are spending time on both the big ideas and the small steps between your regulations and the people you aim to reach. Quite often between your policy and the public is a government contractor. How the government buys things makes all the difference as to whether the benefits you designed actually reach people.

If you are a policy expert, you must understand, in your bones, how your policy is delivered to the public. If you are a food security expert, try filling out the form for food assistance. When you get stuck, call the help number provided on the form. Did you get the help you needed? Did getting that help take a reasonable amount of time? It is never a waste of time to experience what your policy is like for the humans trying to use it. Taking yourself through the policy can only enrich your understanding of how to help the people you are trying to serve.

The next generation of big ideas will fail if they are not grounded in close observation of how the previous generation of public policies reached people, or didn't. We need to move beyond assessing programs via a simple quantitative cost/benefit analysis and modernize our ability to see how people use programs—or don't—through real-time data collection. Then we need to test improvements, look at the data again, and test again.

Policy making for a country of 300 million people in fifty states is a very big enterprise. It is not feasible to talk to and connect with every person. But as we have shown, there are ways of using data to identify different groups of people who represent millions of others. Reaching out to those groups through user research is the modern equivalent of opening the door to Lincoln's White House.

The methods detailed in this book seek to shorten the distance between the public and the policy makers who serve them. Public interest technologists can close this chasm by creating the ability to test, seeing what people need and use, and improving along the way. But at its core, we think this work's highest value is in transforming not only how we deliver government but how we design the policies of the future. As is oft said, "Every system is perfectly designed to get the results it gets."[43] If we want a different set of results, we need to redesign the system.

5

How We Got Here and
Where We're Going

IN THE PRECEDING CHAPTERS we have shared stories about teams in and around government who are embracing an approach to problem solving. These stories are not isolated incidents of people happening upon the same approach by chance. They are part of a growing practice that builds on other movements, some emerging and some that have been around for decades. It is important to understand the evolution of the practice and how it fits into the public policy landscape in order to best unlock its potential for effectively serving people in the digital age.

It is entirely possible that you are familiar with some of the approaches in this book; maybe you are even, unbeknownst to yourself, a member of this fledgling field, but have never heard the term "public interest technology." That is because it is a new invention, spurred by the need to assign a name to the style of work used by specific teams in government and nonprofits. The inspiration for the name "public interest technology" comes from public interest law.[1] By investing in "public interest law" in the 1970s, funders such as the Ford Foundation were able to fill a public sector need for law school graduates to serve the public good. Three decades later, the Ford Foundation began investing in growing the field of public interest technology the way they had done years earlier with law.

The Origins of Public Interest Technology

Though the name for the field is new, along with the concept that the approaches we have discussed in this book add up to a cohesive practice of problem solving, many of the techniques are decades old. Public interest technology overlaps with and builds upon "civic tech" or "gov tech"—related phrases used by practitioners and the media over the past decade—particularly in reference to people working in or around government with a focus on using technology and some of the adjacent practices we've described in this book.

One notable difference between civic tech, gov tech, and public interest technology is the meaning of the word "technology." Civic tech and gov tech are, by definition, technology dependent, in that they cannot exist without some element that adheres to the way we think of technology today—a cloud-based tool, a big mainframe system, a machine learning algorithm. Public interest technology, conversely, refers more broadly to a style of thinking that has evolved along with the development of modern technology—a methodology that begins with end users, employs data to measure progress, and iterates in small segments before reaching scale.

"Civic tech" refers to an early movement aiming to bring transparency and technology into government and the civic sector.[2] There have been organizations focused on the intersection of modern technology and the public interest dating back to at least the 1980s with nonprofits like Computer Professionals for Social Responsibility (CPSR) and, in the 1990s, the Electronic Frontier Foundation (EFF). But the modern field of public interest technology draws a more direct line from the civic tech movement of the early 2000s, with the birth of the Personal Democracy Forum. A notable aspect of civic tech is that civic technologists are often working outside of or adjacent to government, and using open data or other tools to pressure government to be more responsive to citizens. In the past decade or so this term has expanded to include technologists working inside of government, but it still maintains a bit of outsider hacker patina, which is why we have opted not to use the term. However, public interest technology would not exist without the groundwork laid by civic tech.

Going back a bit further in time, the civic tech movement builds on earlier ideas like open government and open data. The concept of open government evolved in the post–World War II United States, spurring the passage of the Freedom of Information Act in 1966. The idea that the government's actions should be public and available to all, especially the press, drove the creation of the legislation. When President Lyndon Johnson signed it into law he noted "a deep sense of pride that the United States is an open society in which the people's right to know is cherished and guarded."[3]

The concept of open government expanded dramatically in the United States after the resignation of President Richard Nixon, with new efforts put in place to hold the government accountable.[4] Decades later, under President Barack Obama's 2009 Open Government Directive, agencies were ordered to make information publicly available online.[5] At the same time, the open data movement began championing the creation of data sets in a format that would allow them to be used by modern technologies like Google Maps.[6] The open data movement is in part an effort to increase government transparency, and it is global. In 2009, the British nonprofit mySociety won in their efforts to require members of Parliament to report expenses to the public.[7]

Open data allows citizens to see the workings of their governments—for better or worse. The Police Data Initiative, established in the wake of the killing of Michael Brown by police in Ferguson, Missouri, pushed 100 police chiefs to commit to data transparency and agree to release police data. At its core, open data is about government publishing data in a way that can be used by others—by citizens to hold government accountable, by nonprofits or companies using living applications or data visualizations to tell a story.

In their essay "The New Ambiguity of 'Open Government,'" Harlan Yu and David G. Robinson argue that open government is a policy, while open data is a technology. One, they note, does not dictate the other. "A government can provide open data on politically neutral topics even as it remains deeply opaque and unaccountable. The Hungarian cities of Budapest and Szeged, for example, both provide online, machine-readable transit schedules, allowing Google Maps to route users on local trips. Such data is both open and governmental, but has no bearing on the Hungarian government's troubling lack of accountability. The data may be opening up, but the country itself is sliding into authoritarianism."[8]

Over the past two decades, technological improvements in generating data have given the government the ability to compile and use data in a way it hasn't before. In the 1990s, efforts to use data to improve services led to the use of "dashboards" and real-time data systems like CitiStat and StateStat. CitiStat began in Baltimore, a city with rampant absenteeism among city staff; the program was designed to tackle that issue.[9]

From 2010 to 2020 many government agencies saw the need for in-house data scientists or chief data officers. In 2011 Chicago became the first city to name a chief data officer. The same year New York City launched its data unit.[10] In 2014 Los Angeles appointed former Code for America alumnus Abhi Nemani as the city's first chief data officer. By 2018, more than two dozen cities and governments had chief data officers.[11] This isn't just a city trend. In 2015 President Obama named DJ Patil the first chief data scientist of the United States.

The data movement has grown rapidly—a 2018 study of mayors found that 49 percent had dedicated staff with roles focused on data.[12] State and city networks of these data chiefs have begun to share best practices, including the Civic Analytics Network[13] and more recently a State Chief Data Officers network.[14] In 2015 Bloomberg Philanthropies launched What Works Cities, an effort that has brought open data, evidence, and innovation tools to over 100 American cities.[15]

More recently, we have seen what happens when government tries to reverse course on open data. In May 2020, Florida governor Ron DeSantis fired Rebekka Jones, the state's top data scientist at the Department of Health, after she refused to manipulate the state's COVID numbers to support reopening the economy. The firing made national news, and Jones went on to launch her own data dashboard.[16]

A parallel field in government is that of gov tech. This field has been around as a concept long enough for it to have spawned an eponymous magazine and multiple conferences, most notably the National Association of State CIOs (NASCIO), where state chief information officers gather annually. Gov tech refers broadly to the use of technology in government, but it also tends to connote the traditional government technology as the public experiences it. Which is to say, giant mainframe systems, a lack of awareness of what it's like to be an end user—all of the approaches we are trying to move away from in this book.

To give a sense of what this field is currently like, NASCIO was formed in 1969 as the National Association for State Information Systems. In 2020, their list of top state CIO priorities included cybersecurity first and digital government second. Under digital government, "improving citizen experience" is listed next to "portal" and "chatbots."[17] No one using a public interest technology approach to problem solving would list chatbots as a top priority, for all of the reasons we have discussed already involving focusing on technology rather than user needs. The field is also not particularly representational of the people working in government. Of fifty CIOs, eight are women[18] and twelve are people of color. Many work their way up through government IT departments, which don't tend to expose people to modern technology practices.[19]

To be fair, for a long time the job of the CIO, and therefore the gov tech field, focused on simply getting the IT in government to function. Do people have e-mail? Can they log on to the network? That focus has shifted over the years as technology has infiltrated more and more of our lives, but in some parts of government getting e-mail to function securely is still part of the CIO's portfolio of work, leaving little time for people-focused problem solving.

Reinventing Reinvention

The idea of modernizing and remaking government is also not a new one. The Census Bureau was historically focused on new inventions that could help it to fulfill its basic responsibilities. In 1890, the bureau pioneered the use of the Hollerith machine, an electric tabulating machine, to speed up counting and reduce costs. The machine was invented by a former Census Bureau employee and was so revolutionary that it was adopted by the

private sector.[20] In 1979 a group of local leaders, sick of ineffi-
ciencies at the local level, started the Alliance for Innovation, a
network of city and county leaders who shared ideas on effective governance. To this day the Alliance for Innovation serves
more than two hundred communities.

And in 1992, David Osborne and Ted Gaebler published the
now-classic *Reinventing Government*, which argued for bringing
business practices of the era such as identifying customer needs
or the concept of "learning organizations" into government.
The book was a best seller and led to an eight-year effort in the
Clinton administration to improve the federal bureaucracy, as
well as the creation of the President's Management Council,[21]
an interagency effort to get government officials to focus on
management measures, which is still in use today.

Though the concept of "modernization" may not be new, the
world is not the same place it was in 1993, when *Reinventing Government* hit the shelves. In the intervening years, the Internet and
smartphones have been invented, and the way business is done
has changed dramatically. Stephen Goldsmith, Neil Kleiman, and
Steve Case recently brought this reinvention work into the digital
age with their city-focused work *A New City O/S: The Power of
Open, Collaborative, and Distributed Governance.*[22]

Public interest technology as a field is still somewhat amor-
phous. Does a start-up using an app to donate water to Africa
count as public interest technology? What about a public works
department applying behavioral nudges to increase recycling?
What about an NGO or private company using technology to
help families sign up for federal food assistance? Building a
movement typically requires naming it and explaining what it
is, but perhaps this effort is unnecessarily complex for public
interest technology. The most important part, we believe, is the
doing. We need more doing.

Public Interest Technology Today

There are a significant and growing number of teams who would agree that their work and the approaches they take fall within the field. Globally, Canada, the United Kingdom, India, Australia, Finland, Estonia, Mexico, Denmark, Italy, and many other countries have national-level teams devoted to innovation and digital governance. The World Bank and the United Nations have been pioneering this approach as well. At the federal level in the United States, USDS and 18F bring technical expertise and a public interest technology approach to multiple federal agencies. At the state level, there are fledgling digital service teams in California, New Jersey, Colorado, North Dakota, Florida, and New York whose stated goal is to work on improved digital service delivery. Multiple cities have formed similar teams under a variety of names, including San Francisco's Office of Civic Innovation, New York's Office of Economic Opportunity, the District of Columbia's Lab@DC, Philadelphia's Design Lab, and many more.

In some cases cities began by establishing an innovation team, or hiring one or two data scientists or customer experience designers into an agency and then growing their ranks and practice from there. Other agencies are still working to bring on their first hire. Still others were spurred to change from business-as-usual via a project brought to them through an outside entity, as in the stories we shared of Vermont's Integrated Benefits Initiative project, Rhode Island's foster care work, or Michigan's improved benefits application. In California, an external reform effort to improve CalFresh, California's food assistance program, was led by individuals—Alan Williams and Dave Guarino—and supported by Code for America over the course of six years.[23]

In governments and nonprofits, the shape that public interest technology takes and how it is integrated into organizations is quite varied. Sometimes it looks like an entirely new office that didn't previously exist; sometimes it starts with a new role or builds into an office that has data or technology embedded in its mission. Of the stories we've shared in this book, no two use exactly the same model to make change happen.

Anchoring Transformation in Existing Technical Teams

In some cases, an existing tech-focused team evolves to also be the innovation team. In Asheville, North Carolina, digital services director Eric Jackson worked to change the IT department's reputation. "We're not the typical IT department of 'no,'" he told us. "Our primary orientation is, 'How can we get you what you want?'"[24] That's helped make other departments feel more comfortable bringing ideas to him, and has led to citywide projects that benefit multiple departments.

As CTO of New Orleans, getting e-mail up and running was task number one for Lamar Gardere: "When we would try something new, folks would say, 'Okay, that's great, but why doesn't e-mail work?' There wasn't an opportunity to do anything beyond the basics until we mastered the basics."[25] Mastering the basics won the IT team the trust of other agencies across the city, which gave them the opportunity to dig into city issues beyond e-mail. They started with open data and eventually moved to developing human-centered services.

In the case of both Asheville and New Orleans, because the IT team was already positioned as a cross-governmental, cross-agency entity, with hard work and strong leadership, teams parlayed standard IT projects into service design work.

Creating an Entirely New Team

Bloomberg i-team grants, offered through Bloomberg Philanthropies, provide funds for individual cities to establish small
teams focused on solving a specific issue, which may span multiple agencies or departments. These teams work to dig to the
bottom of issues including reducing blight, improving economic outcomes for people returning from jail, or reducing the
murder rate. I-team members have reorganized entire city departments; redesigned forms, stickers, and notices; rewritten
call center scripts; used free tools to capture data or coordinate
agencies; and in one case amended the state constitution.
Whatever a team deems is necessary to solve a problem, they
figure out how to get done. These teams are highly focused. By
chipping away at a single problem for years, they often make
significant progress.

In Boston, the New Urban Mechanics team started as an in-
cubator for new ideas in 2010. Over the years they've grown to
assist multiple departments with specific problems. Austin,
Texas, uses a similar model, working with agencies as varied as
the convention center and the recycling center. The team also
runs a citywide certification program on content strategy and
user research. The value of this model is that work is centralized
in one location. Because the same team works on innovation
efforts across the city, they can apply what they've learned or
built for one agency to the next project with a different agency.

Expanding the Tool Kit across an Organization

While having a dedicated person or team focused on data or problem solving is often helpful, true transformation is a whole-
government effort. Government leaders, management experts,

and data reformers we interviewed for this book made clear that long, sustained change can't be done by a few new data or innovation staffers—it requires systems change. One way that both cities and states and agencies spread these public problem-solving techniques is to spread the practices and make new tools available.

Charlotte, North Carolina, has a strong culture of using data going back decades. When the team was charged with launching a citywide data portal[26] to house the city's large number of data sets, they quickly realized they couldn't do it alone. They decided to offer help before they asked for help, by launching what they call OpEx Academy—a training school for city employees, run by city employees, to share skills on data. To date, city employees from departments as varied as police to parks have engaged in over sixty-five courses of peer-led training.

We spoke to one twenty-year veteran of city employment who described connecting with other city staff working on data and learning new skills as "the best experience in my entire career." Investing in building skills of existing city staff was an essential ingredient in getting departments to share data on a central portal, according to Rebecca Hefner, the data and analytics officer for the city. It was also a great way to launch a data movement across the city government. While the Center for Data Analytics has a handful of staff members, OpEx alumni are now a cadre of hundreds of data leaders citywide.

Charlotte isn't alone in its approach to investing deeply in existing city staff. Other cities such as San Francisco and Denver have established robust efforts to include the use of data to improve outcomes as a part of everyone's job, not just the work of a chief data officer or special innovation team. Denver has pioneered improvement using "lean" methods through its own city training effort, aptly named Peak Academy.[27]

New York City has several teams and departments with a focus on improving services, including the Mayor's Office of Economic Opportunity. That team worked well within their own agency, but they wanted to figure out a way to serve other parts of the city. They had run design studio workshops with other agencies. They had also developed a tool kit on human-centered design that they made available across the city. But they were looking for something lightweight to do every week to support people's efforts to incorporate user research, proto-typing, agile development, and other standard innovation elements. Ultimately, the team hit on the idea of offering office hours for anyone in any city agency to walk through the Service Design Studio door and get help.

The office hour idea was a shot in the dark—the team had no idea if anyone would sign up, or what kind of requests people might come in with. "We had no idea what we were getting into," Mari Nakano, the office's design director, says.[28] But they quickly found themselves overwhelmed with bookings. As of early June 2020, they've held 250 office hours with thirty-four unique agencies, for a total of nearly 500 attendees. The office hours have been so successful that they've been getting meeting requests from people outside New York City government—to date they've held office hours with thirty-three other governments, including Rhode Island, California, Denmark, and Tai-wan. The team is still relatively new, so they have limited data on whether their involvement has positively influenced projects, but they are tracking repeat visitors to hours and workshops, goals and outcomes of projects discussed in each session, satisfaction rates, and what types of questions people come to sessions with. In the three years they've been holding hours, they've seen questions shift from learning about their tools and tactics to discussing specific projects or requests for assistance in achieving stakeholder buy-in.

In Orlando the innovation team runs a three-day academy that takes frontline city employees through a rapid prototyping and testing workshop for forms specific to their agency. Staff members pair up with people from other departments to walk through their service—for example, someone from the Parks Department might try to report a pothole. At the end of the three days, the team launches a user-tested beta site. The innovation team is systematically working through all 350 city services. As of this writing they've met with teams from 300 city services, and are also measuring Orlando residents' trust in government based on their interactions with those services.[29]

The Obama administration experimented with a federal model for cross-agency work called Community Solutions, anchored by a single team embedded in the Office of Management and Budget (OMB). This effort worked to improve federal agency collaboration in serving communities in distress. Over 1,500 federal employees from across a dozen agencies were trained to get closer to the field where programs were implemented and to work across silos.

Nonprofits Using New Methods

While we see government transformation as the key practice of this book, this work also exists in the nonprofit sector. Code for America is one of the leading organizations to advance the practice of improving government delivery in the United States. Founded in 2009 by Jennifer Pahlka, the work of CfA has changed and transformed over time, but at its essence, CfA works to improve government services at scale. They have done this by supporting fellowships, brigades of local civic techies, and enterprise projects to model what improved delivery looks like. CfA also holds the closest thing to a family reunion for public technologists, the Code for America Summit, an annual event where leaders in the work share practices. In 2019 the conference drew over 1,000 people. Similarly, for a slightly different subset of the public interest technology world, the Personal Democracy Forum has brought the field together annually since 2004 to discuss technology's impact on society.[30]

There are many other nonprofits and companies who use technology to improve government services, including Benefit Data Trust, Benefit Kitchen, mRelief, and Propel. Others are using human-centered design, data, and implementation sciences to improve the delivery of their own work, such as the Creative Reaction Lab, the Institute for Health Improvement, Harambee Youth Employment Accelerator, and Participle, based in the UK. A public interest technology upgrade to the tool kits of the world's nonprofits would have a profound impact on their ability to serve needy populations.

Organizations and Programs Aiming to Cultivate These Skills

In order for the field to fully develop, it is not enough for organizations and governments to change how they approach problem solving; we must also incorporate these methods into how we train future public servants. A number of fellowships and programs exist to help governments, universities, and organizations do just that. Additionally, there are networks and philanthropies working to provide a clear pathway from academia to public interest technology jobs.

In 2019, New America (the think tank where we both work), in collaboration with the Ford Foundation, launched the Public

Interest Technology University Network (PIT-UN) with twenty-one universities in an effort to bring a public interest technology mindset to computer science and public policy students alike. Now in its second year, the network has thirty-six member universities. PIT-UN brings a multidisciplinary approach to teaching policy, with member schools offering classes that explore foundational topics such as security, privacy, ethics, data, and design thinking.

Numerous philanthropic entities and nonprofits are also investing in skills building, data systems improvement, and technology for the public good. The Partnership for Public Service has outlined strategies aimed at improving the ability of governments to recruit tech talent.[31] DataKind places top-flight data scientists into nonprofits. Data4BlackLives works to bring the power of data to organizations addressing racial justice. FUSE Corps is another highly effective fellowship that brings midcareer managers into the public sector to work on thorny problems. The Tech Talent Project works to recruit tech leaders into government, and TechCongress has been doing yeoman's work to recruit midcareer tech leaders to do a "tour of duty" in congressional offices. In our program at New America, we have worked with area-specific nonprofits like UnidosUS and the Asian and Pacific Islander American Health Forum to mentor them on building an in-house technology practice, and incorporating a public interest technology approach in solving their specific problems and meeting their members' needs. And more broadly, several centers, nonprofits, and foundations have developed efforts to place public interest technologists in nonprofits and governments.

Universities are also working to house public interest technology efforts. The Beeck Center for Social Impact and Innovation at Georgetown University has begun to become a university home for scholars on digital government. Harvard University has a number of collaborations aimed at assisting government leaders in building skills on data and delivery.[32] Globally, Inez Mergel at the Universitat Konstanz leads efforts to upgrade the public administration teaching playbook. And Tom Steinberg, who was instrumental in the birth of GDS in the UK, leads a group of academics on improving the teaching of digital practices to public servants.[33]

———

The work of expanding a field is ever-changing. Sometimes it feels like every day there is a new public interest technology effort in a different corner of the world. It is thrilling to see, but it means we cannot possibly provide a comprehensive list of the field. We have attempted to cover some of the major players here, and to share the different ways that governments and nonprofits are incorporating public interest technology into their work. We have also provided a resource guide at the end of the book for those who would like to dive in further and get involved.

6

Public Interest Technology in Practice

THUS FAR, we have shared examples that illustrate why public interest technology is important, and why it is crucial that policy makers and government leaders think differently about how to approach problem solving. But we don't want to give readers the impression that applying these methods is simple or fast. In this chapter we'll show what the work is like on the ground.

The Work Is Slow

While we may all love exciting, splashy stories, the majority of innovation and modernization in government doesn't look like that.[1] The slow pace can be a huge source of frustration for problem solvers who live in a world where everything keeps getting faster but who work in a job where time itself can seem to stand still. The dire needs of constituents served by government compound frustration with the slow pace.

Practitioners come to do these jobs because they are deeply committed to change, and their work is imperative to improving the real lives of the people who the government serves. It's painful to know you have the intellectual, technical, and resource capacity to improve a parent's ability to feed their children, but you can't press "go" until you get two heads of agencies that don't work together in the same room, and the negotiation to do so takes five months. To that end, many of the stories we have shared in this book were multiyear efforts. And once a new process, tool, or system launches, the work is not done. Public interest technology relies on iteratively taking the pulse of how well public needs are being met via data and research. We don't live in a static world, so those needs are ever changing. A solution that worked well five years ago may not be the right solution today. Once practitioners have carved out space and established pipelines to put the data, design, and delivery methods we've discussed into practice, the work of iterating becomes easier and faster. But getting there is no small feat.

Support from the Top

There is not one single story in this book where the person at the very top—the mayor, the governor, an agency head—did not vigorously champion the project. It isn't news to say that change comes from the top, but in the case of public interest technology, the changes that need to happen can be so all-encompassing and such a divergence from how work usually gets done that senior-level champions become essential. It is not enough for the person at the top to say sure, that sounds fine to me. This person must be a true believer who paves the way and removes any blockers (of which there will be many) before they arise.

In Germany, the state secretary at the Ministry of Finance, Wolfgang Schmidt, told us that he reads correspondence the ministry is sending out to constituents to make sure it strikes a helpful tone.[2] He also personally dug into why Germany's financial need form was twenty pages long and how it could be reduced. A leader who is willing to worry about the details of delivery is essential to public interest technology.

Schmidt says that he learned to get into the details from his boss, the German finance minister Olaf Scholz, who does the same. "I've been working with him for eighteen years now, and, obviously, I adopted his style a little bit. He is very much into the details. At the same time he is a strategic thinker, but then he can be a pain in the ass when it comes to details and really going into the substance of things. He sometimes drives people in his ministry crazy who are not used to that."[3]

Support from the top means more than having someone in a leadership position who likes your team and gives you a budget. It requires that they empower the team to operate differently. This sometimes means that teams align with a mayor's passion, as with Bloomberg i-teams, or New York City's Office of Economic Opportunity. But for teams everywhere, support from the top means the space to fail, the ability to walk into offices where they might not be wanted and try something new, and the political power to hack through the bureaucracy, redesign departments, jobs, and processes, and make change.

James Anderson, head of government innovation at Bloomberg Philanthropies and former advisor to Mayor Bloomberg, put it this way: "If you want to get big things done in the public sector, you need serious, sustained executive leadership. The mandate for change comes from the top. The push to keep working through bureaucratic resistance and turf wars comes from the top. The tiresome, unsexy slog of implementation, evaluation, and iteration requires encouragement and sunlight from the top."[4]

Support from the top also means that there is someone willing to take the fall when things go badly. Nigel Jacob, who has run Boston's New Urban Mechanics (NUM) team since 2010, said that early on in his tenure he noticed that people seemed afraid to do things differently, so he dug into the underlying reasons. It wasn't that they were afraid of taking risks or failing. What they were really afraid of, it turned out, was the nasty phone call from the mayor or the press or even their peers that inevitably came when things didn't go as planned. Jacob's team solved the problem by bringing any project they worked on under the NUM umbrella, which meant that if there was a nasty call in the offing, it came to Jacobs or one of his team members rather than to a specific department.

Support from the Ground Up

Support from the top isn't enough without support from the people on the ground. In Vermont's benefits work, it was essential to the success of the project that the caseworkers in the Barre office were not only on board with the project, but were excited about it. Because ultimately, the project relied on caseworkers changing their daily tasks in order to succeed. The Vermont team had been very careful in how they approached the Barre caseworkers, bringing them along step by step so that nothing was a surprise when it was finally unveiled.

In Civilla's work in Michigan, research with frontline state agency staff led to the discovery that the process wasn't working for anyone—not those it was meant to serve and not the frontline workers for Michigan's Department of Health and Human Services (MDHHS). The insights from the government workers were as valuable as the insights from the beneficiaries. The transformation that ultimately happened was not possible without deep involvement throughout the department, from the top to the front lines. If the frontline workers had been left out of the design process, those insights would have been missing.

And ultimately, the success of the project came down to a sense of ownership by the staff who needed to incorporate the changes into their daily work lives.

In *Reinventing Organizations*, Frédéric Laloux eloquently describes this frontline or bottom-up engagement in vision, problem-solving, and ownership. He cites numerous organizations achieving this distributed responsibility, including Buurtzorg.[5]

Buurtzorg, the home care entity based in the Netherlands, is built on this model of distributed responsibility. The model is simple: Cut out the middle managers and empower nurses who are most connected to patients. The organization has tremendous outcomes, with high rates of patient satisfaction and health outcomes, but their model is essentially a tech-enabled return to the empowered neighborhood nurses of yesterday.

Culture Matters

As office culture in the private sector, especially the tech sector, has changed to include free snacks, casual attire, hotelling rather than dedicated desks, and nap rooms, it has become another area where the gulf between the private sector and the public sector has become chasm-like. When a public sector employee walks into a private sector building, it often feels like there is money and luxury oozing out of the walls. All of the things people take for granted in the private sector, like endlessly refillable free coffee, open workspaces, and whiteboards, are often nowhere to be found in government buildings. These are only the physical trappings of the work environment, but they are symbolic of all the ways in which government has been starved for resources and challenged to keep up. Many government office buildings look like you've accidentally walked into 1965. Comparatively, the average tech start-up looks like a spaceship.

We are not suggesting that government offices must include nap rooms in order to use modern problem-solving methods, but one theme that came through as we spoke with public interest technology pioneers was that culture matters. In our interviews, business process experts, system engineers, data scientists, and agency leaders from across the globe went out of their way to make this point.

Martha Lane Fox, who was a fundamental puzzle piece in the UK's effort to launch its Government Digital Service, told us that she felt GDS would have been more effective had they done more on the cultural change front. "Even though we had levers from the center, I didn't do enough to bring the whole civil service along," Fox told us. "You have to build culture. Everyone can have a role to play."[6]

After decades of doing this work, David Osborne observed that public interest technology methods only make a big difference if "the purpose, power structure and accountability system, the culture, and the relationship with customers" have also changed. The internal culture must shift from one of compliance and fraud prevention to one driven by a mission to serve and help people.[7]

Not Yet of, by, and for the People

Go to a government technology or innovation conference and look around. You'll see that the majority of attendees tend to be white and male. In 2015 women made up 22 percent of the U.S. government tech workforce, while white men made up over 50 percent. White workers make up about 70 percent.[8] The numbers are even more lopsided at the highest levels of tech companies.[9]

Although women are underrepresented in technology, they make up a growing portion of the civic innovation workforce. On New York City's Design and Product Team within the Mayor's Office for Economic Opportunity, for example, six of the ten staff members are women. More broadly, within the leadership team for the Office of Economic Opportunity, six of ten directors are women. USDS staff is 50 percent female, and the leadership is over 60 percent female. Code for America's staff consists of 65 percent women/nonbinary, with 76 percent women/gender nonbinary on the leadership team. And our own public interest technology team at New America is run by a staff of all women, half of whom are women of color.

Despite the prevalence of women in the field, a hard look suggests that we have a long way to go at making the demography of the field match the demography of the United States, but even more so in drawing leaders from the communities they serve. We heard from numerous practitioners in public interest technology that diversity of all kinds is integral to appropriately designing services for people. Vivian Graubard, one of the founding members of USDS, discovered that her background as a Spanish-speaking first-generation American gave her insight into her immigration policy work that the rest of the team didn't have.

The USDS team was building a new system, and Graubard felt strongly, based on her personal experience, that it should exist in Spanish, as the majority of users would be native Spanish speakers.

"I have family members who speak English, but it's not their first language," she explains. "The complicated legalese of what you're asking them is just beyond where they're comfortable. I understand what people are going through when they're using these systems—they are nervous. They don't want to answer the question incorrectly. They don't want to sign their name to something that could be wrong and then send it to the U.S. government. So it matters that they really understand what question they're being asked."[10]

In New York City, a diverse set of perspectives on the team meant a better understanding of data on multiple projects. In 2017, the city decided to bulk up their long-standing fight against rats. By tapping into 311 call center data, the team figured they could pinpoint where the worst rat problems were in the city and target their efforts there. But when Amen Ra Mashariki, the chief analytics officer in the Mayor's Office of Data and Analytics (MODA), looked at the data, he immediately saw a problem. Mashariki had grown up in a public housing project in the Bedford-Stuyvesant section of Brooklyn and still lived in the neighborhood. When he came home late at night from the mayor's office, he saw rats scurrying about. So when he first got the 311 data, he did the normal thing you would do when looking at data—he looked at his own neighborhood.

"I thought, that's really weird," Mashariki recalls.[11]

According to the data, there wasn't much of a rat problem in Bed-Stuy. No matter which way his team sliced the data, it kept showing very few rats in the neighborhoods Mashariki knew from personal experience were rat-infested.

Mashariki called up an old friend who still lived in the projects and asked what had happened to all of the rats. According to the city's data, he explained, there were no more rats there. His friend laughed. There were plenty of rats, he assured Mashariki. "Then why doesn't anyone call 311 to complain?" asked Mashariki.

"What's 311?" his friend replied.

This story illustrates not only the importance of validating where your data comes from—study after study has shown that wealthier white people are more likely to lodge complaints with 311[12]—but also why the people parsing the data need to represent a variety of perspectives. Had Mashariki not grown up in a primarily low-income neighborhood he might not have seen the gaps in the 311 data. But thanks to his background and curiosity, he was able to bring a perspective to the project that was sorely needed. Mashariki found blind spots in the data and elevated how neutral-seeming data of one type can amplify the voices of some over others. Because the public interest technology field, in its current state, skews white, it is important for practitioners to be aware how the makeup of their team might affect the interpretation and application of that data. The tools we've described must be designed and driven by humans with a breadth of perspectives. They have the power to amplify our best or our worst traits—technology can be used to expose implicit bias and racism in our data collection, or to perpetuate it.

Yet, it's not Mashariki's responsibility alone to consider the context in which social problems exist because he happens to have been raised in a poor neighborhood. The onus is on anyone who works with data sets to consider the limits of what those numbers can tell us about the lived experiences of the people they represent. A well-trained technologist from any background should be armed with the skills and knowledge to ask the types of questions Mashariki asked. That's part of the training we hope to see happen for those who enter this field.

Diverse backgrounds have always been important in public problem solving. When a cholera epidemic gripped 1830s London, the source was a mystery. At first glance, Dr. John Snow was an unlikely person to locate the source. He was a big-shot doctor who attended to Queen Victoria during several of her births. The cholera epidemic was largely confined to poor neighborhoods, so most doctors blamed the outbreak on the perceived filthy habits of the lowest classes. But while Snow's work had taken him to Buckingham Palace, he had grown up, and continued to live, just a few blocks from the center of the epidemic.

"The poor were dying in disproportionate numbers not because they suffered from moral failings," he wrote. "They were dying because they were being poisoned."[13]

Snow went on to map the outbreak data and traced the source to a contaminated well. Being "from the neighborhood" was as relevant to problem solving in Victorian London as it is now.

"Yes, we have some diversity in policy. We'll have certain senior leadership places in city government that focus on diverse initiatives, immigration, so on and so forth, that require diversity," Mashariki says. "But there's almost little to none in the tech space. Diversity isn't just getting a young African American man from Iowa. If you're the city government in New York City, diversity is getting someone who grew up in the projects to be a part of it. That's a level of diversity that we almost never hit."[14]

The 311 data story isn't the only time Mashariki noticed that something was off with the data he was being shown. At the time, the city's homeless shelters were full, and because New York is legally required to give shelter to anyone who demonstrates a need, the Department of Homeless Services (DHS) found themselves scrambling for more space. In an effort to find more space for the city's homeless population, DHS began giving out vouchers that people experiencing homelessness could trade for a room in a house. In exchange, DHS paid the homeowners $1,000 a month. DHS handed the vouchers out at shelters to try to free up space, but there were surprisingly few takers. Why, the agency wondered, wouldn't someone jump at the chance to leave a city shelter for a private home?

Having Data Is Not Enough

The city brought on a consulting agency to look into the problem. The consultants looked at the data and determined that, for whatever reason, people simply did not want to take the vouchers. This didn't sit right with Mashariki. It happened that his older brother worked at a nonprofit that ran several shelters in Brooklyn, so he picked up the phone to ask his brother why people weren't taking the vouchers.

His brother told him there were three reasons people weren't using all the vouchers. The first was that the vouchers only covered housing.

"When you're in a shelter," his brother told him, "you get three hots and a cot. When you get a room, you get a bed and are on your own with food."[15]

The second problem was that not all vouchers were equal in the eyes of the recipients. Some were for upscale neighborhoods where voucher recipients could barely afford the price of water. Some were for rooms that were far from where people might have kids in school or an elderly parent they were caring for. The prime neighborhood vouchers—Manhattan and Brooklyn—went first. But finding takers for the vouchers in Staten Island was impossible.

"People act like those in need can't be choosy, but yes, they can," says Mashariki. "They have a right to be choosy and say, 'I don't really want to move to Staten Island. I don't want to have to take a two-hour train to the Bronx when my mom lives in Brooklyn.' But what gets tagged in the data is, we offered this voucher to this person, but they didn't take it."[16]

The last factor his brother listed was the timing of when vouchers were offered. If they didn't get to shelter residents right away, the residents would start to settle into the shelter, meet people, and become a part of the community. That meant the last thing they wanted to do was pick up and move somewhere else. But if the vouchers were offered within a day or two of arrival, new shelter arrivals were more likely to take them. None of this information was reflected in the data.

"What was key, most important for us to think about whenever we had a data set, was not what kind of analysis can we do with the data, but what is missing in this data?" Mashariki concludes. "I need to first find out what I don't have."[17]

Many organizations have data, but having data is not enough. Data needs to be the right kind, and put to use in meaningful ways. The leaders and organizations featured in this book are using real-time, distortion-resistant data to better understand problems and how to fix them.

"When I came to government I saw the federal CIO's offices have these IT project dashboards for high risk projects, and they're all green, all the time," Mikey Dickerson recounts. "Except for one exception, which is when a particular agency is lobbying for an increase in budget, then it will turn yellow for that year because they need more money. Otherwise it's green at all times."[18]

The data reflected in the dashboards Dickerson saw was all self-reported. And because people's job performance evaluations were tied to the data, everyone reported that everything was going along swimmingly—until a crisis arrived, like the launch of Healthcare.gov, at which point people discovered that the data they were gathering didn't mean anything.

W. Edwards Deming taught the use of data in his "plan, do, study, act," a systematic process for learning and continuous improvement. The model relies on asking three questions: What are we trying to accomplish, how will we know a change is an improvement, and what changes can we make that will result in an improvement?

Deming's process, sometimes referred to as the Model for Improvement, became ubiquitous in the 1980s corporate world and is still a fixture at business schools. Today's data collection tools might be more sophisticated than in Deming's era,[19] but the core approach of asking questions and using data to test what works remains essentially the same.

Data on its own provides only the *what*. In order to understand what the data is actually saying, it is important to speak with end users to learn the *why*. Data used in this way becomes a constant feedback loop between people and policy makers or program managers. It informs problem solvers about who needs what, and whether they are getting those needs met.

Similarly, interviews with end users also only provide a portion of the full picture. In order to verify what people are telling you, to understand the scope of a problem, or to understand how the problems you hear in user interviews translate into who does what when (or doesn't, as the case may be), the interviews need to be correlated with data.

Data also provides an excellent starting point for formulating questions. In the homeless voucher data, the only thing the data revealed was that people weren't using the vouchers at the anticipated level. The team could have made all kinds of assumptions about what was happening with the vouchers, but the simplest, most accurate way to dig into the numbers was to call up a shelter and ask why. Never be afraid to ask why. That advice goes for digging deeper on data that might be missing or even for asking the basics in a meetings. So often everyone in the meeting is wondering about some basic question that no one asks. Never be afraid to ask why or get clarification. Chances are you are not the only person wondering.

When Public Interest Technology Does Harm

For the public interest technology field to flourish it needs to grow with true intentionality toward representing the people it aims to serve. The risks of misusing technology or incomplete data in the public sector are exponentially greater than the risks of building a product for only one segment of the population. If a product start-up fails, so what? If the government fails, people go bankrupt, become homeless, or worse.

As we have discussed, layering technology over a broken process is a recipe for failure. But layering technology over an unjust policy has the potential to speed up the application of the policy. The field's most notorious examples of harm come from algorithmic biases, which have been well documented, but are also only the tip of the iceberg.

In Michigan, from 2013 to 2015 over 50,000 people were wrongly denied their unemployment benefits by an algorithm that was found to be wrong 93 percent of the time.[20] The Michigan Integrated Data Automated System (MiDAS) was built by a private company and cost $47 million to implement. One part of its failure was that it relied on a single data point for fraud detection. Whenever there was a discrepancy between data reported by claimants and their former employers, the system always assumed that the employee was wrong. An automated questionnaire was sent to those with this data discrepancy, and if information was not received by the agency within ten days (even if the questionnaire went to the wrong address), the system made a determination that the employee had committed fraud. A fraud determination meant a 400 percent penalty payment on the unemployment check plus a 12 percent interest markup. As a result the state garnished taxes and wages to pay the fine, and people lost their homes. This misuse of data caused

tremendous harm to thousands of families who sought help
they had earned through paying into unemployment benefits.

But beyond the faulty algorithm lies another, larger problem
that has not gotten nearly as much attention: unemployment insurance is often rotten at the core. In our team's work digging into
how unemployment insurance systems function, we learned that
when unemployment insurance was first envisioned by the government, it codified racist practices by omitting jobs that were
more likely to be held by people of color.[21] That practice contin-
ues to this day. Making it function better and faster only amplifies
the structural inequities that are baked into the system.

So consider this a warning label for the public interest technology processes we've outlined in this book. Because public
interest technology aims to make things easier for users, speed
processes for government, and ultimately make government
and policies more effective, there is always the possibility that
these strategies can be used to do great harm. Historically, governments around the world, including in the United States,
have been responsible for significant atrocities and injustices.
As we were finishing up this book we learned that the United
States Immigration Customs and Enforcement agency (ICE)
had been accused of performing unneeded hysterectomies on
immigrants.[22] So even though public interest technologists
might undertake this work with the best of intentions, without
excavating the underlying structures beneath policy, they run
the risk of exacerbating inequalities, or worse.

The people we spoke with in the field were acutely aware of
the potential for data misuse, and many had spent time working
through possible ways things could go wrong should they implement the proposed changes for their given project. Data
sharing agreements among local tax and health and human service agencies to help people get their benefits more efficiently
could, for example, be used by another set of leaders to track

family immigration services. It is imperative to have this conversation, and to design for an unknown future, where the people who make these decisions may not be you.

But it is equally important that practitioners in the field perform due diligence on existing policies before undertaking new projects. Public interest technology's focus on delivery means considering who has been least served in the past and digging down to the root cause. It is not enough to improve an existing process. We must also actively deconstruct the processes that have failed people in the past.

———

The emerging field of public interest technology is young. It has had and will likely continue to have growing pains where the movement fumbles before fixing and improving itself while moving toward a more representative or sustainable version of its ideals.

While today's field leaders suggested that there is no "perfect cookie recipe" for building this work correctly, there are some ingredients that every recipe needs: a focus on users, data instrumentation, and the ability to learn and adapt quickly. Many suggested that they can't predict the work of tomorrow, but they all acknowledged that constant adaptation over time is imperative.

"I think that the future of the field is that it becomes integral to governing," Todd Park told us. "Public interest tech expertise can benefit work on virtually every major challenge and opportunity in front of us, helping frame the right questions and helping inform and shape optimal solutions. It'll be really exciting to see what leaders and innovators do to get more and more public interest tech savvy into the work of public service in all of its forms, across all domains."[23]

7

Growing the Practice of Public Interest Technology

FIELDS DO NOT MIRACULOUSLY transform and modernize overnight. In *The Great Influenza*, John M. Barry's recounting of the 1918 influenza pandemic, Barry notes that the field of medicine remained unchanged for two millennia.

"In 1800 Hippocrates and Galen would have recognized and largely agreed with most medical practice," Barry writes.[1]

Since the time of the ancient Greeks, medicine relied largely on observation and reasoning rather than experimentation. The breakthrough that brought about a seismic shift for the field was the study of pathological anatomy, which correlated treatments with results in order to determine whether the treatment had been effective. Autopsies and dissection unlocked details and revealed correlations that before doctors could only guess at. In some sense, in this book we propose a similar shift in the science of problem solving. Rather than guessing at the problems that exist and theorizing how to solve them, public interest technologists must dissect, apply a treatment, and test to see if it works.

In *Reinventing Government*, Osborne and Gaebler offered readers a vision of government as it might be, and concluded with the following: "Our governments are in deep trouble today. In government after government and public system after public system, reinvention is the only option left. . . . We hope that the vision we have laid out will unlock the remaining gates—unleashing a paradigm shift throughout American government."[2]

If government was in deep trouble then, in 1992, pre-pandemic, pre-2020 economic crisis, before incident after incident of police brutality toward Black Americans (over 1,000 in 2020 alone), in a world where business moved at the speed of the fax machine, just think where we must be today.

Transforming bureaucracies from Anchorage, Alaska, to Kalamazoo, Michigan, to Manchester, England, will demand changes to the way many governments work today. People will need to work in new ways, governments will need to hire differently, and the public sector will need to embrace a culture that rewards collaboration and sharing across agencies, sectors, and locales. There is transformative work already under way that does all of the above in places large and small. Some of these stories are described in the previous chapters; many more are not. But the good work happening today is a drop in the ocean of how most governments and nonprofits function. To make the kind of change required to scale the work described in this book will take a lot of little and big actions. So where do we begin? Two clear starting points are telling the story of this work and investing in the field and the people who do the work.

Storytelling

First, we need to make visible *how* we work, not just what we work on. For the past several years we have been focused on telling these kinds of stories in order to grow the work, because we know that public information technology spreads via exposure.

Leaders in one city or agency might hear how a similar city or agency improved their services and wonder, Why can't we do that here? We saw this at work with a story Hana wrote for *Fast Company* about work on blight in Mobile, Alabama. Minutes after the story went live, residents from Augusta, Georgia, to Johannesburg, South Africa, asked on social media whether similar projects could work in their towns.

But this also wasn't your usual government story, rooted in failure or overreach. There is a clear hunger for stories on solving common problems through smart government work, borne out by the high readership numbers we've seen when these kinds of stories go live. But because these stories don't fall into any traditional reporting beat—they're sometimes tech stories, but more typically they are stories of government functioning as it should, which isn't the type of story that normally makes headlines or draws clicks—they are underreported. In addition, the work can be all-consuming, with practitioners often finding themselves barely coming up for air between projects, which means there isn't much in the way of outreach in the field. No one is pausing from counting street homelessness in their city to send out a few press releases.

Much of this work is unseen—fixing something that is tedious, speeding up a slow process, making sure that government works the way it said it would—so telling the story of the work is critical to the continued success and growth of the field. Teams need to be actively pitching their work, cultivating relationships with reporters, or bringing a communications specialist onto their team. We know of a lot of wonderful, inspiring, untold stories in the field. Some of them are in this book. For every 100 stories of government being broken, there are many others of how it is working, but far fewer of them are told.

Investing in People

We need to reward, recruit, and lift up the leaders—in government, the private sector, and nonprofits—who are experimenting with new ways of working and getting results. We also need to reward leaders who put an end to practices that don't produce outcomes. Finally, we need to produce more of these kinds of leaders.

Throughout history, there have been people who are motivated by making change in their community or the world at large. The Peace Corps, the Volunteers in Service to America (VISTA), Teach for America, AmeriCorps Seniors, and AmeriCorps were all founded on this principle. Hordes of college graduates come out of university wanting to make a difference. Will these graduates make as much working for the government as they would at a start-up app that rates cute hamsters and finds them rides? No, of course not. Will they do meaningful work that affects large numbers of people's lives? Yes. And often, once people get a taste of the impact they can have in government, they're hooked.

"I've made something to help people find bus routes that might make their day five seconds easier. But it's like 10,000 people whose days are five seconds easier because of that," says Brendan Babb, the chief innovation officer of Anchorage, Alaska. "That is really addictive."[3]

What is lacking is not people who fit this mold but jobs that meet their criteria, which is where investment comes in. With funding, government can also up its game on public sector hiring, training, and salaries.

Mikey Dickerson told us that if he had three shots at improving government, he would spend all of them on recruiting, hiring, retention, incentives, rewards, and promotions: "You need ways to reward success that are better than we have right now. You need ways to attract people that are better than we have right now. If you want to make government better you need to improve your hiring and your people management processes."[4]

As we noted earlier, public sector salaries have not kept pace with the private sector. While government has never been the path to fortune, the hollowing of government budgets since the 1970s has changed the nature of public sector employment. In the United States, the pay for some jobs that used to be a ticket to the middle class, especially for teachers and police, is so low it requires a second job to make ends meet. This isn't true worldwide. Some countries invest deeply in their public sector and pay people well. Being a government worker or school-teacher in these locales carries prestige and a good paycheck. In other periods of American history, we have called upon citizens' patriotism and sense of community to ask them to serve in government or to step up and make, build, and save as a country. The Works Projects Administration in 1935 employed millions of Americans during the Depression who in turn built the physical infrastructure of the country, including 650,000 miles of roads, 8,000 parks, and 16,000 miles of new water lines.[5] There is no reason the current recession couldn't produce a more technologically driven New Deal of innovation and reinvention.

Rebranding Government and Investing in the Field

It would be unusual to meet an undergraduate from a top university who aspires to work in the civil service. Even at the school that was founded to be the premier training ground for future government leaders—the Harvard Kennedy School of Government

(HKS)—a third of graduates take private sector jobs.[6] A decade ago the school removed "government" from its name.

In an article about HKS's shifting focus in *Boston Magazine*, Carol Chetkovich, a professor of public policy at Mills College who researches public policy school training, said she found "a decline in stated interest in government careers" after completion of training and that "a large proportion of students went to the private sector at that point. I was really struck by the level of skepticism and disdain that respondents expressed toward government."[7] Tara's public policy graduate students at Georgetown often express an enthusiastic interest in working for the public sector, but have a hard time breaking in, and many take jobs with nonprofits while waiting to hear back for government roles.

Government used to be seen as a reasonable, secure place to work. It guaranteed you a job, an income, and a pension. In the 1950s, 5 percent of the workforce was employed by the federal government.[8] People were invested in their communities, and because those jobs meant a solid career path and economic security, they were also seen as respectable ways to provide for one's family.

Today, top graduates do not necessarily think, "Oh, boy, when I graduate I'm going to go work for the city!" And if by some chance they do, they will soon discover that the amount of time it takes to get a government job and the salary on offer are not even remotely comparable to the private sector. While consultancies that work with the government, like Deloitte or Booz Allen Hamilton, offer training, career paths, and solid middle-class starting salaries and allow grads to start work shortly after they complete school, often the government has none of that to offer.

Training in government, in the United States, is nothing like the investments made in individuals in many private sector companies or like the training investments many countries make internationally in civil servants. The amount of time from a job offer to a start date can sometimes stretch over a year. And job applicants often need to pass a civil service exam before they can even apply to work for their city. In previous eras, passing the civil service exam was seen as a ticket to a good job. Today it feels like a relic from a different time.

While many of these hiring challenges are logistical, the public's general mistrust of government does not help. Americans' trust in government—and in many cases trust in governments around the world—has never been lower, and who can blame them? Governments globally have been captured by special interests, and while wages have been stagnant for many, the cost of living has risen, and so has inequity. People see the government as working for someone else—companies, banks, wealthy people. In response to the coronavirus, the federal government failed to protect people and left much of the population to fend for themselves. At the state level, unemployment websites from Michigan to Florida crashed under the crush of new applications. U.S. government leaders can't agree on the right approach to dealing with a pandemic, let alone how to help their scared, sick, or broke constituents. In the United States, centuries after the end of slavery, deep, pernicious structural racism persists. The U.S. government has been unresponsive in seeking justice for the countless murders of Black Americans by police. Now more than ever we are reminded that there are things we cannot do alone, things we need government for.

This may be the best time of all to appeal to a new generation of leaders to come help their governments. What better time to spur people into action than at a moment of utter dysfunction and chaos?

For those who have made the transition from private sector to public sector, the experience is something like a religious awakening. Todd Park, who has become something of a professional public interest technology evangelizer, found himself at a loss for words as he reflected back on his time in public service: "Working in public service was an honor and a privilege that I can't even begin to describe in words—it's so meaningful, and it's so inspirational, and it's so hard."[9]

Park also remembers a time when people found it unthinkable that they might be able to recruit workers away from the tech sector.

He recalls, "When we started, people said, 'Well, maybe you'll get twenty other crazy people to leave their multimillion-dollar stock options, packages, and free sushi to go work for the VA in DC.' And through the incredibly hard work of a bunch of folks, we got 200 people to show up, and they were the very, very, very best of the best."[10]

In a speech to a generation of technologists at the SXSW Conference in March 2015, Mikey Dickerson made the choice for future pioneers clear: "Some of you, not all of you, are working right now on another app for people to share pictures of food or a social network for dogs. I am here to tell you that your country has a better use for your talents."[11]

We, too, are here to tell you that the public sector needs you even more than it did in 2015. The work of solving problems at scale isn't going to magically get done by others. People need to come into government and nonprofits and do the work. It is hard to say whether there has ever been a more urgent moment to solve problems. At this critical time, the work of public interest technology can mean life or death for millions of citizens. Do not leave this work up to someone else.

Our problems are not unsolvable. This book is full of people already doing the impossible—ending homelessness, reaching millions of people with life-saving behavioral health interventions, transforming systems that allow access to citizenship and rights and guarantees. We have provided you with a guide to taking a public interest technology approach to solving problems, making policy, and eliciting change in the world around you. It is now up to you to use it. The future depends upon it.

AFTERWORD

Anne-Marie Slaughter
Darren Walker

THE FORD FOUNDATION SUPPORTS "visionary leaders and organizations on the frontlines of social change." Tara McGuinness and Hana Schank fit the bill, as do the women and men they write about so compellingly in these pages: Marina Nitze, who collaborated with the state of Rhode Island to clear an eighteen-month backlog of foster care placements in a weekend; Michael Brennan and Adam and Lena Selzer, cofounders of Civilla, who worked with the state of Michigan to reduce the length of the form that residents must fill out to apply for unified benefits by 80 percent, from a daylong process to twenty minutes, dramatically increasing the number of fully and accurately completed forms, reducing the burden on caseworkers, and speeding the flow of benefits; or Jos de Blok, who revolutionized community nursing in the Netherlands.

Many of these leaders have been practicing public interest technology without necessarily using the term or recognizing the concept. A great contribution of this book is to bring many disparate people and organizations together under a common rubric, one that both pulls together existing work and pushes us all to think about "technology" as much more than the shorthand we use to refer to a piece of digital hardware or software.

In its widest sense, technology refers to the application of scientific knowledge for practical purposes, or, more colloquially, the transformation of research into tools. Public interest technology, as McGuinness and Schank define it, brings together multiple strands of science around design, data, and delivery and applies them to the solution of public problems. That process of application, in turn, is, in their words, a *practice*, a "new practice . . . that better positions organizations to be responsive problem solvers."

The definition of public interest technology adopted by the Public Interest Technology University Network is similar: "The study and application of technology expertise to advance the public interest, generate public benefits, and/or advance the public good." It is not accidental that this definition is emerging now. Like the emergence of Black American studies, ethnic studies, and women's studies in the 1960s and 1970s, all of which sought to redress a paucity in scholarship about groups deemed to be on the margins of society, public interest technology offers a counterweight to dominant narratives about who technologists are, what they make, and whom they make it for.

More concretely, public interest technology offers us a framework from which to consider how to advance and protect human rights in a digital world. It argues for a systematic way of studying technology in the world—including unforeseen and adverse consequences. And it offers us new language and vocabulary with which to understand how technological tools and innovations may impede and erode hard-fought rights won and gained from the early nineteenth century through the twentieth century. As mass protests swept through the United States during the summer of 2020, we not only heard cries for the right to breathe and exist, but for the right to not be surveilled or attacked through technological weaponry.

A Brief Historical Excursion

To understand the full value and potential of where we are, it's necessary to go back a bit. We are both international lawyers by training; we both came of age as public interest law was becoming not only a field but an indispensable part of any good law school's curriculum and career offerings. The creation of that field was not accidental; it was spurred and funded by philanthropy, with the Ford Foundation in the lead. We both thus quickly saw an analogy, even if an imperfect one, between public interest law and public interest technology.

Back in 2013, many years before the work of intentionally marrying the fields of technology and public interest began and this emerging field of PIT had a name, the Ford Foundation was struggling and failing to find sufficient and culturally appropriate technologists to work with grantees. As foundation staff researched the problem, they found it to be similar to so many challenges arising from the enormous technical transformation sweeping through parts of the world. So Ford took the challenge to its peers as the focus of the first-ever NetGain collaboration.

NetGain was an attempt to pick a few large, complex, structural technology-driven problems that all foundations were grappling with and to wrestle with them together, president to president, as a means of developing smarter solutions. In this collective spirit, the MacArthur, Open Society, Mozilla, Knight, and Ford Foundations agreed that the first NetGain Challenge should focus on what they called "the tech talent pipeline." Further research revealed that even though more students were graduating with computer science degrees than ever before in history, very few of these computer scientists would find their way into a career path beyond academic research or the private sector. Even fewer of them had the training to wield their technological knowledge in service of addressing social problems.

The foundations commissioned Freedman Consulting to create a framing document for their discussion. The resulting report, *A Future of Failure? The Flow of Technology Talent into Government and Civil Society,* documented the structural barriers that were keeping technical talent off a pathway to public service. NetGain presidents used that document as a road map for several shared grants that directly addressed some of the identified gaps. They funded fellowships to civil society and government, interdisciplinary courses between computer science and law schools, peer-reviewed journals so that public interest technologist academics could publish, and professional development opportunities. These grants made clear the mammoth scope of the challenge ahead, but also the reward in solving it.

Freedman's second report, *A Pivotal Moment: Developing a New Generation of Technologists for the Public Interest,* came with a set of twenty-six recommended "interventions" for foundations and individual philanthropists to consider on the demand side, the supply side, and the marketplace to grow the field of public interest technology. Reading that report, Anne-Marie was inspired to write a grant proposal designed specifically to "enable individual technologists to plug into a larger system—a set of educational and career pathways that reinforce one another and add up to a larger whole." This book helps define the parameters of that larger ecosystem.

A final report, *Building the Future: Educating Tomorrow's Leaders in an Era of Rapid Technological Change,* built a blueprint for universities to break down silos between the technological- and the humanities-based programs to develop technologists who would be more effective in different environments such as civil society and government. The report suggested that we needed educational programs that would prepare individuals to be able to move back and forth across different communities of practice, mixing and matching different disciplinary traditions. A convening with twenty-five university presidents led to the establishment of the Public Interest Technology University Network. That network, discussed below, is now thirty-six universities strong, all of which are legitimizing, expanding, and professionalizing a practice that historically had been the work of outliers.

As McGuinness and Schank make abundantly clear, the public interest technology ecosystem depends on many different hubs: not only specifically tech-focused organizations like Code for America and Civic Hall, both of which have been indispensable to building this field, but also a host of organizations that do *not* think of themselves as tech-oriented but that use the design-data-delivery approach. That broadening of both the definition of technology and of the category of organizations and individuals who use it is critical for the further development of the field.

The Public Interest Technology University Network

A key piece of the PIT ecosystem is the university and college pipeline. PIT-UN launched in March 2019 with twenty-one charter members: Arizona State University, Carnegie Mellon University, the City University of New York, Columbia University in the city of New York, Florida International University, Georgetown University, Georgia Institute of Technology, Harvard University, Howard University, the Massachusetts Institute of Technology, Miami Dade College, Olin College of Engineering, Pardee

RAND Graduate School, Pepperdine University, Princeton University, Stanford University, the University of California, Berkeley, the University of Chicago, the University of Michigan, the University of Texas at Austin, and the University of Virginia.

As of this writing, we have thirty-six members. The network is the spine of a growing community of practice: a group of faculty members and administrators who meet regularly to share their innovations—new courses, internships, student and community projects, certificates offered, and programs created. Listening in on these calls is a rare opportunity to watch field building in practice. To hear about how

- MIT's Schwarzman College of Computing, UVA's School of Data Science, and UC Berkeley's Division of Data Science and Information (DDSI) are all creating multidisciplinary spaces where computer and data scientists will interact with ethicists, philosophers, humanists, and social scientists to explore their ethical and social responsibilities in a wider context.
- The Pardee RAND Graduate School has completely revamped its curriculum to train students in three broad areas of policy engagement: research, analysis, and design; community-partnered policy and action; and technology applications and implications.
- The University of Chicago has pioneered a two-year master's degree in computational analysis and public policy; Arizona State University (ASU) has created a master's of science in public interest technology. Many other universities have created new degrees and certificates to combine science, particularly computer and data science, and public policy.
- Carnegie Mellon University, Georgia Tech, UT Austin, Harvard University, and others are aiming to foster a

culture of interdisciplinary work without creating new academic infrastructure. They have done this through creating nontenure public interest technology roles and integrating public interest modules and principles into their teaching and research.

- Miami Dade College and CUNY's College of Staten Island are creating a direct pipeline of course work and experiences for high school students of color to prepare them for associate and bachelor's degrees in PIT-focused majors.

- Florida International University, Carnegie Mellon University, Olin College of Engineering, Princeton, and Stanford University have created fellowship and internship programs for both graduate and undergraduate students to use applied, tested digital service methods to help solve problems during their placement in government and local organizations.

- Georgetown, Pepperdine, and Arizona State universities offer opportunities for midcareer professionals in government to enhance and upgrade skills. Georgetown is piloting replicable workshops on AI & Ethics for those working at the intersection of technology and policy, while Pepperdine and ASU offer weekend-based certificate and master's degree programs for those seeking to learn about the latest technological tools they can use to make local governments more transparent, inclusive, and responsive to the residents they serve.

- The University of Texas and the University of Michigan cohosted the first of what they hope will be an annual undergraduate PIT conference to rotate across their institutions.

- Howard University, in partnership with Georgetown and Stanford, leads an effort to capture case study narratives of past public interest technology projects, so that others may learn from PIT-UN members and build upon their successes.

These institutions see public interest technology as an interdisciplinary endeavor that places the welfare of society at its center. They seek to engage a cross section of disciplines to determine how to prevent technology from exploiting the structural and institutional barriers that erode the rights and advancement of its most vulnerable citizens.

Looking Forward

Think tanks emerged on the policy landscape roughly a century ago to provide "good government" solutions to difficult social and economic problems. They have traditionally hired lawyers, economists, and PhD- or master's-level experts in fields like education, environment, labor, housing, and national security. Today, in think tanks, government offices, and civic organizations, we need a technologist at every problem-solving table. Not necessarily—or even mostly—to create or recommend a technological solution, but to bring a tech mindset—an engineer's, designer's, or data scientist's mindset—to the problem at hand.

We believe an essential element of advancing social justice is ensuring that technology is a force for public good. At Ford the entire foundation's work has been transformed by our learnings in the public interest technologist sphere. In the fall of 2016 Ford began hiring technology fellows to work in each of the foundation's program areas. The aim is not only to bring a tech lens to the foundation's work but also to cultivate a generation of tech leaders equipped to use technology to challenge inequality in all its forms and expand inclusion and opportunity.

This wonderful book makes the best possible case for why and how we need to transform our understanding of what public problem solving is about and how we need to reinvent government to build the capacity necessary to tackle problems at scale. But McGuinness and Schank are the first to recognize how far we have to go. As they write in the final chapter, "The good work happening today is a drop in the ocean of how most governments and nonprofits function. To make the kind of change required to scale the work described in this book will take a lot of little and big actions. So where do we begin?"

They argue for storytelling and investing in people, both of which are essential. We would add a number of additional proposals, many of which build on work that is already ongoing, but which outline an even bolder vision.

1. *A Cornucopia of Academic Opportunity.* Every university or college that offers a policy track of some kind—whether a certificate, a major, an advanced degree in policy, public and international affairs, or public administration—should have a tech track within it, as prominent and well funded as the economics track. The University of Chicago's MA in computational science and public policy is a great example, as is ASU's MS in public interest technology.

2. *A Digital National Service Corps.* In the summer of 2020, amid the pandemic and the massive economic crisis, proposals surfaced for a Digital Works Progress Administration, modeled on the New Deal program that paid people across the country to go to work on government projects. Now imagine that we finally pass a law requiring all young people, and encouraging all people, to devote a year of their lives to national service, either

physical or virtual. Those who chose the virtual track could get their first taste of public interest technology. Over the course of the year they would be able to take webinars and trainings introducing them to all sorts of public interest tech opportunities in multiple sectors.

3. *From CPA to CPIT.* Like public interest lawyers, public interest technologists would see themselves as part of a licensed profession with a mission of service and advocacy in technological innovation. They would be public problem solvers specifically skilled in design, data, and delivery. It should be possible to set up a global entity to license them, one that would begin by defining criteria that could be met both by education and above all by service hours.

4. *A Civic Hall in Every City.* Civic Hall in New York City is a space where community activists, practitioners, and scholars meet. Many would define themselves as part of the civic tech movement pulled together by Code for America, the Personal Democracy Forum, and other hubs for young people committed to using technology in the public interest. We need more of these spaces, which can serve as a kind of tech public square. They should have common membership criteria, mission statements, and programming, even if they take different forms and are funded differently in their respective communities. But they should aim to provide a meeting place to bridge government and civil society initiatives in the broader service of public interest technology.

5. *A Black Tech Ecosystem.* The for-profit technology companies are overwhelmingly white, which makes them uniquely unsuited to serve a plurality country in which no one ethnic or racial group has a majority. It is

essential, particularly for public interest technology, that we build entire ecosystems of technologists of color, starting with Dr. Fallon Wilson's idea of a Black Tech Ecosystem. To fund this ecosystem, just as we fund any innovation, we need multiple investment funds— venture capital, impact funds, angel investors, funding collaboratives—to invest specifically in Black technologists and technologists from other communities of color.

We hope that professors in all the universities and colleges listed above and many more will assign *Power to the Public* as the first book on the syllabus for any course exploring how technology can be used in the public interest. We hope that college and university presidents will choose it as a first-year pre-read. We hope that nonprofit organizations, from think tanks to community advocacy and service providers, will recommend it as a must-read for their staff. We hope that aspiring politicians at every level, from the school board to the cabinet, will read it and reimagine what government can do and how it must do it. We hope it will be a requirement for anyone wishing to take the civil and foreign service exams, for both federal and state government.

People throughout the United States and around the world need hope and belief in our collective capacity *to solve problems*. Indeed, in many countries we need to forge a new social contract with our governments: to provide health, justice, liberty, equality, safety, and prosperity through new and far more equitable systems. For all who seek to engage in this work, *Power to the Public* is both a manual and a manifesto.

ACKNOWLEDGMENTS

THIS BOOK WOULD NOT HAVE come into existence without the public interest technologists and problem solvers who get up every day and do the hard work of shining a light into the darkness, seeing what is possible, and making it a reality. Thank you for giving us something hopeful to write about.

We also owe an immeasurable debt of gratitude to those who not only cleared the way for public interest technology as a field, but who made the space for us to write this book, provided this work a home at New America, and cheered us along the way. This book would not be in your hands without the hard work of Anne-Marie Slaughter, Cecilia Muñoz, Vivian Graubard, Andreen Soley, Elizabeth Garlow, Vontisha Fludd, Jenny Toomey, Darren Walker and the Ford Foundation, Reid Hoffman, and Todd Park.

Peter Dougherty, our editor, read an article about public interest technology and thought the topic might make a good book. Thank you for your vision, your guidance, your humor and your wisdom. Thank you to our reviewers and to Princeton University Press for organizing them—it is no small feat to find peers in a nascent field. Their thoughtful reading and comments strengthened this book.

Most of the people we interviewed for this book found time to speak to us during a global pandemic while working from the kitchen counter, often with young children tugging at their sleeves, or otherwise in a general state of chaos. We cannot thank you enough for that. We learned so much from each of you.

Many people helped us find the pioneers we feature in these pages. Thank you to Jethro Sercombe for cluing us in to the wonderful work of Buurtzorg, Zoe Blumenfeld for connecting us with the Vermont Integrated Benefits team, and Ginny Hunt for explaining how the benefits work survived past her tenure at USDS. Thank you to the teams at Civilla, Crisis Text Line, USDS, Code for America, the Beeck Center, Community Solutions, 18F, and Nava Public Benefits Corp.

We had planned to travel in researching this book, but when coronavirus abruptly put a halt to those plans, we had to find other ways to learn about project details and local color. Thank you to Andrea Gibbs for helping us paint a picture of Rockford, Illinois, through the years. Thank you to the ROOST at Rittenhouse for letting us check in early and stay late and for supplying us with multiple glass containers of coffee beans. And to the Highlights Foundation, thank you for always being the perfect place to write and edit.

This would not be a book about technology without a few technical hiccups. Thanks to Ben Damman for whipping up a quick script so we could get the manuscript from Google Docs to Word with all of our footnotes intact.

So very many thanks to Alexandra Hohenlohe, our New America intern and super researcher, who worked her way through a list of research needs that we thought would take all summer in her first two weeks, allowing us to get even deeper into our research.

From Hana:
Thank you to my father, Roger Schank, who told me to say yes to everything and figure out how to do it later. And to Diane

Schank, my mother, who still reads everything I write. Thanks to Milo and Mira for gamely participating in constant dinner table conversations about this book and the stories in it. I think "PIT Stop" is a great title. And finally, thanks to Steven Shaklan, who shows me every day what it looks like to care deeply about others.

From Tara:

Thank you, dear Nora and Grace. You are my world. You remind me of the fun, spirit, and possibility of the next generation of problem solvers every day. And a special thanks to Damian Murphy, who is never daunted by the world's challenges, big or small, and always encourages me to go for it. Finally, thanks, Mom and Dad, for taking care of all of us, all the time.

NOTES

Preface

1. Tom Freedman et al., *A Pivotal Moment: Developing a New Generation of Technologists for the Public Interest*, Freedman Consulting, LLC, May 2016, http://tfreedmanconsulting.com/wp-content/uploads/2016/05/pivotalmoment.pdf; Tom Freedman, Sam Gill, and Alexander Hart, *A Future of Failure? The Flow of Technology Talent into Government and Civil Society—A Report*, Freedman Consulting, LLC, 2013, https://www.fordfoundation.org/media/1893/afutureoffailure.pdf.

2. "The White House," Mr. Lincoln's White House (The Lehrman Institute), accessed June 29, 2020, http://www.mrlincolnswhitehouse.org/the-white-house/.

3. Was Rahman, "Starbucks Isn't a Coffee Business—It's a Data Tech Company," Marker, January 16, 2020, https://marker.medium.com/starbucks-isnt-a-coffee-company-its-a-data-technology-business-ddd9b397d83e.

4. Jennifer Pahlka, "Delivery-Driven Government: Principles and Practices for Government in the Digital Age," Medium.com, May 30, 2018, https://medium.com/code-for-america/delivery-driven-government-67e698c57c7b.

5. W. Edwards Deming, *The New Economics for Industry, Government, and Education* (Cambridge, MA: MIT Press, 1993).

6. "Our Ideas," Carnegie Foundation for the Advancement of Teaching, accessed September 26, 2020, https://www.carnegiefoundation.org/our-ideas/.

Chapter 1

1. John Roth, "USCIS Automation of Immigration Benefits Processing Remains Ineffective," 2016, https://www.oig.dhs.gov/reports/2016-03/uscis-automation-immigration-benefits-processing-remains-ineffective/oig-16-48.

2. Sean Alfano, "Technology Blossoms in 2005," CBS News, December 29, 2005, https://www.cbsnews.com/news/technology-blossoms-in-2005/.

3. "NHS IT System One of 'Worst Fiascos Ever,' Say MPs," BBC News, September 18, 2013, https://www.bbc.com/news/uk-politics-24130684.

4. Brian Jackson, "Phoenix Failure Will Cost Government $2.2 Billion: Senate," IT World Canada, August 1, 2018, https://www.itworldcanada.com/article/phoenix-failure-will-cost-government-2-2-billion-senate/407636.

5. Katherine Gregg, "UHIP Debacle: R.I. to Extend Contract, as Deloitte Agrees to More Concessions," *Providence Journal*, March 15, 2019, https://www.providencejournal.com/news/20190315/uhip-debacle-ri-to-extend-contract-as-deloitte-agrees-to-more-concessions.

6. Mark Schwartz, phone interview by authors, January 15, 2020.

7. Kenneth C. Gilliland, "Recompeting a Services Contract: Common Issues in Dealing with an Incumbent," *Journal of Contract Management*, July 2014, http://read.nxtbook.com/ncma/contractmanagement/july2014/recompetingservcontract_feat.html.

8. Brian Lefler, phone interview by authors, January 3, 2020.

9. In researching this book we talked to nonprofit and government staff of varying seniority and experience, ranging from political appointees to frontline workers. Many civil servants we spoke with were not able to speak with us on the record, especially the more junior ones. We have tried to represent their views in this book even though we were not able to use names or quotes.

10. Schwartz interview, January 15, 2020.

11. Ibid.

12. Eric Hysen, phone interview with authors, December 10, 2019.

13. Roth, "USCIS Automation of Immigration Benefits."

14. Hysen interview, December 10, 2019.

15. Lefler interview, January 3, 2020.

16. Vivian Graubard, phone interview by authors, June 26, 2020.

17. Dana Chisnell, phone interview with authors, December 6, 2019.

18. Ibid.

19. ELIS Field Office, conversation with author, July 13, 2016.

20. Author analysis of research conducted at multiple ELIS processing centers (unpublished internal report prepared September 2016).

21. Schwartz interview, January 15, 2020.

22. Léon Rodriguez, phone interview by authors, January 16, 2020. All other quotations from Rodriguez in this chapter are sourced from this interview.

23. Rodriguez interview, January 16, 2020.

24. *Federal IT Modernization: How the Coronavirus Exposed Outdated Systems*, 116th Cong. (2020) (testimony of Hana Schank), House Committee on Oversight and Reform, Government Operations Subcommittee.

25. "Naturalization Fact Sheet," U.S. Citizenship and Immigration Services, 2019, https://www.uscis.gov/news/news-releases/naturalization-fact-sheet.

26. Andy McCarthy, "A Brief Passage in U.S. Immigration History," New York Public Library, July 1, 2016, https://www.nypl.org/blog/2016/07/01/us-immigration-history.

27. Jeremy Rifkin, *The Zero Marginal Cost Society: The Internet of Things, the Collaborative Commons, and the Eclipse of Capitalism*, rev. ed. (New York: Griffin, 2015).

28. Esri StoryMaps Team, "The Age of Megacities," *National Geographic*, June 4, 2020, http://admin.nationalgeographic.org/interactive/age-megacities/; "U.S. and World Population Clock," U.S. Census Bureau, accessed June 30, 2020, https://www.census.gov/popclock/.

29. "National Intercensal Tables: 1900–1990," 2016, U.S. Census Bureau, https://www.census.gov/data/tables/time-series/demo/popest/pre-1980-national.html.

30. Evan Osnos, "Can Mark Zuckerberg Fix Facebook before It Breaks Democracy?," *New Yorker*, September 10, 2018, https://www.newyorker.com/magazine/2018/09/17/can-mark-zuckerberg-fix-facebook-before-it-breaks-democracy.

31. Ibid.

32. Yuri van Geest, "Exponential Organizations" (PowerPoint presentation, October 20, 2014), slide 15, https://www.slideshare.net/vangeest/exponential-organizations-h.

33. United States Army Service Forces, *Annual Report*, 1945, https://www.archives.gov/research/guide-fed-records/groups/160.html.

34. Michael D. Bordo, Claudia Goldin, and Eugene N. White, *The Defining Moment: The Great Depression and the American Economy in the Twentieth Century* (Chicago: University of Chicago Press, 1998), chap. 4, p. 130, https://www.nber.org/chapters/c6891.pdf.

35. Van Geest, "Exponential Organizations," slide 12.

36. Michael Zhang, "A Brief History of Kodak: The Rise and Fall of a Camera Giant," PetaPixel, June 14, 2018, https://petapixel.com/2018/06/14/a-brief-history-of-kodak-the-camera-giants-rise-and-fall/.

37. U.S. Citizenship and Immigration Services, "USCIS Makes Another Form Available for Online Filing," press release, October 30, 2019, https://www.uscis.gov/news/news-releases/uscis-makes-another-form-available-online-filing.

38. Michael Land, phone interview by authors, February 19, 2020.

Chapter 2

1. Tara McGuinness and Anne-Marie Slaughter, "The New Practice of Public Problem Solving," *Stanford Social Innovation Review*, Spring 2019, https://ssir.org/articles/entry/the_new_practice_of_public_problem_solving.

2. Joel Kurth, "Michigan Tames a 18,409-Word Testament to Bureaucracy Run Amok," *Bridge Michigan*, February 1, 2018, https://www.bridgemi.com/michigan-government/michigan-tames-18409-word-testament-bureaucracy-run-amok.

3. Ibid.

4. Michael Brennan, phone interview by authors, December 17, 2019.

5. Ibid.

6. Ibid.

7. Lena Selzer, phone interview by authors, December 17, 2019.

8. Gabriela Dorantes, phone interview by authors, September 18, 2020.

9. Selzer interview, December 17, 2019.

10. Interviews with Lena Selzer about original Re:form research and Zack Quaintance, Government Technology (e.Republic, June 2018), https://www.govtech.com/civic/A-Blueprint-for-Human-Centered-Change.html.

11. Dorantes interview, September 18, 2020.

12. "Policy Basics: The Supplemental Nutrition Assistance Program (SNAP)," Center on Budget and Policy Priorities, June 25, 2019, https://www.cbpp.org/research/food-assistance/policy-basics-the-supplemental-nutrition-assistance-program-snap.

13. Dorantes interview, September 18, 2020.

14. Michigan Department of Health and Human Services, "MDHHS-1171 Assistance Application Standards and Guidelines," accessed June 29, 2020, https://s3files.core77.com/files/pdfs/2019/86102/905702_woyqpvNp8.pdf.

15. "Winner, Service Design Award," Core77 Design Awards 2019 (Core77, Inc., 2019), https://designawards.core77.com/Service-Design/86102/Project-Re-Form.

16. Brennan interview, December 17, 2019.

17. Kit Collingwood-Richardson, "Empathy and the Future of Policy Making," Medium, The Fourth Group, May 14, 2018, https://medium.com/foreword/empathy-and-the-future-of-policy-making-7d0bf38abc2d.

18. DJ Patil, phone interview by authors, February 20, 2020.

19. "Winner, Service Design Award."

20. Tom Tullis, "Measuring the User Experience" (presentation, UX Masterclass, Montreal, Canada, September 20, 2010).

21. Pahlka, "Delivery-Driven Government."

22. "The Digital Services Playbook," Digital Services Playbook, accessed June 29, 2020, https://playbook.cio.gov/#play1.

23. Todd Park, Zoom interview by authors, June 30, 2020.

24. Hilary Cottam, e-mail exchange with the authors, September 2020.

25. Alice Gregory, "R U There?," New Yorker, February 9, 2015, https://www.newyorker.com/magazine/2015/02/09/r-u.

26. Reid Hoffman, interview with Nancy Lublin, Masters of Scale, podcast audio, December 3, 2018, https://podcasts.apple.com/tz/podcast/your-plan-b-needs-plan-b-w-nancy-lublin-do-something/id1227971746?i=1000425082268.

27. Kenneth Burke, "107 Texting Statistics That Answer All Your Questions," Text Request, May 24, 2016, https://www.textrequest.com/blog/texting-statistics-answer-questions/.

28. Aaron Smith, "Americans and Text Messaging," Pew Research Center, September 19, 2011, https://www.pewresearch.org/internet/2011/09/19/americans-and-text-messaging/.

29. "Everybody Hurts: The State of Mental Health in America," Crisis Text Line, 2020, https://www.stateofmentalhealth.org/.

30. Ali Watkins, "N.Y.C.'s 911 System Is Overwhelmed. 'I'm Terrified,' a Paramedic Says," New York Times, March 28, 2020, https://www.nytimes.com/2020/03/28/nyregion/nyc-coronavirus-ems.html.

31. "Everybody Hurts."

32. Bob Filbin, phone interview by authors, March 4, 2020

33. Ibid.

34. Paul Clolery, "Lublin Fired, Crisis Text Line Board Apologizes to Staff," Nonprofit Times, June 13, 2020, https://www.thenonprofittimes.com/npt_articles/lublin-fired-crisis-text-line-board-apologizes-to-staff/.

35. "Board and Advisors," Crisis Text Line, accessed July 1, 2020, https://www.crisistextline.org/about-us/board-and-advisors/.

36. "13th Annual State of Agile Report," Digital.ai, May 8, 2020, https://stateofagile.com/#ufh-i-613553418-13th-annual-state-of-agile-report/7027494.

37. Ginny Hunt, phone interview by authors, March 4, 2020.

38. Hana Schank and Sara Hudson, Getting the Work Done: What Government Innovation Really Looks Like, New America, October 16, 2018, https://www.newamerica.org/public-interest-technology/reports/problem-solving-government/.

39. Lena Selzer and Michael Brennan, co-founders of Civilla, phone interviews by authors, December 17, 2019.

40. Cass Madison, phone interview by authors, March 5, 2020.

41. Madison interview, March 5, 2020.

42. Thani Boskailo, phone interview by authors, September 18, 2020.

43. Dorantes interview, September 18, 2020.

44. Genevieve Gaudet, phone interview by authors, February 10, 2020.

45. Ibid.

46. Ibid.

47. Domenic Fichera, phone interview by authors, February 10, 2020.

48. Quoted in email correspondence with Zoe Blumenfeld (Nava), July 7, 2020.

49. Fichera interview, February 10, 2020.

50. Madison interview, March 5, 2020.

51. Fichera interview, February 10, 2020.

52. Gaudet interview, February 10, 2020.

53. Government Digital Service, "Government Design Principles," Gov.uk, 2012, https://www.gov.uk/guidance/government-design-principles.

54. Brennan interview, December 17, 2019.

55. Domenic Fichera, phone interview by authors, September 13, 2020.

56. Morgan True, "Vermont Health Connect Costs Could Hit $200 Million," Vermont Biz, *Vermont Business Magazine*, March 10, 2015, https://www.vermontbiz .com/news/march/vermont-health-connect-costs-could-hit-200-million.

57. Boskailo interview, September 18, 2020.

58. Ibid.

Chapter 3

1. Todd Park, phone interview by authors, June 30, 2020.

2. Mikey Dickerson, phone interview by authors, June 25, 2020.

3. Graubard interview, June 26, 2020.

4. Marina Nitze, phone interview by authors, February 13, 2020.

5. Ibid.

6. Ibid.

7. Marina Nitze, "Rhode Island's Unconventional Approach to Foster Care," New America, June 14, 2018, https://www.newamerica.org/weekly/rhode-islands -unconventional-approach-foster-care/.

8. "The Problem," Foster America, accessed September 27, 2020, https://www .foster-america.org/the-problem.

9. Ibid.

10. Ibid.

11. "Andrew C. v. Raimondo," Children's Rights, accessed June 29, 2020, https:// www.childrensrights.org/class_action/rhode-island/.

12. Nitze, interview, February 13, 2020.

13. Ibid.

14. Ibid.

15. Ibid.

16. Ibid.

17. Ibid.

18. Ibid.

19. "Child Welfare—Legislative History," chap. 11 in *Green Book*, Committee on Ways and Means, U.S. House of Representatives, accessed April 19, 2020, https:// greenbook-waysandmeans.house.gov/2011-green-book/chapter-11-child-welfare /child-welfare-legislative-history.

20. "Concise User's Guide: Microsoft® MS-DOS® 6," Epson (Microsoft Corpora- tion, 1993), https://files.support.epson.com/pdf/dos60_/dos60_u1.pdf.

21. Nitze interview, February 13, 2020.

22. Jos de Blok, Zoom interview by authors, April 8, 2020.

23. "Buurtzorg Web," Buurtzorg, accessed June 29, 2020, https://www.buurtzorg.com/innovation/buurtzorg-web/.

24. Bradford Gray, Dana O. Sarnak, and Jako Burgers, "Home Care by Self-Governing Nursing Teams: The Netherlands' Buurtzorg Model," Commonwealth Fund, May 29, 2015, https://www.commonwealthfund.org/publications/case-study/2015/may/home-care-self-governing-nursing-teams-netherlands-buurtzorg-model.

25. Park interview, June 30, 2020.

Chapter 4

1. "Rockford Lowers Its Sights," *Washington Post*, May 6, 1983, https://www.washingtonpost.com/archive/politics/1983/06/05/rockford-lowers-its-sights/ac370c54-b628-4031-867c-2af4fb1a20e5/.

2. Economic Federal Reserve Bank of St. Louis, "Unemployment Rate in Rockford, IL," accessed November 4, 2020, https://fred.stlouisfed.org/series/ROCK417URN.

3. From conversations with Community Solutions, their by-name list data shows that by October 2015 Rockford was down to eight homeless persons. This was within their functional zero threshold because they were housing at least eight per month. By December 2018, they were down to just two remaining homeless persons. Conversations with Jake Maguire, Angie Walker, and Jennifer Jaeger, September 17, 2020.

4. Julia Parshall and Caitlin Bayer, "Built for Zero Collaborative: Communities Sustaining an End to Homelessness over Time" (presented at National Human Services Data Consortium, 2019 Spring Conference, April 15–17, Nashville, Tennessee), https://nhsdc.org/wp-content/uploads/2019/04/Day2-Session5-Studio7-Communities-Sustaining-an-End-to-Homelessness-Over-Time.pdf.

5. Larry Morrissey, phone interview by authors, May 7, 2020.

6. Cecilia Muñoz, phone interview by authors, April, 9 2020.

7. Ibid.

8. Andrew Greenway, Ben Terrett, Mike Bracken, and Tom Loosemore, *Digital Transformation at Scale: Why the Strategy Is Delivery* (London: London Publishing Partnership, 2018).

9. Code for America, "Delivery-Driven Policy: Policy Designed for the Digital Age," November 2019, p. 2, http://s3-us-west-1.amazonaws.com/codeforamerica-cms1/documents/delivery-driven-policy-code-for-america.pdf.

10. Park interview, June 30, 2020.

11. Quoted in Robert Costa and Philip Rucker, "Trump's $1 Trillion Stimulus Is a Gamble for Reelection—and a Sea Change for Republicans Once Opposed to Bailouts," *Washington Post*, March 18, 2020, https://www.washingtonpost.com /politics/trump-coronavirus-economic-stimulus-reelection-bailout/2020/03/18 /280a1a12-6947-11ea-9923-57073adce27c_story.html.

12. John Cassidy, "The Good, the Bad, and the Ugly in the Two-Trillion-Dollar Stimulus," *New Yorker*, March 26, 2020, https://www.newyorker.com/news/our -columnists/the-good-the-bad-and-the-ugly-in-the-two-trillion-dollar-stimulus.

13. "United States Conference of Mayors Requests $250 Billion in Localized Aid to Fight Virus, Maintain City Services, Help Workers and Local Businesses," PR Newswire, March 18, 2020, https://www.prnewswire.com/news-releases/united-states -conference-of-mayors-requests-250-billion-in-localized-aid-to-fight-virus-maintain -city-services-help-workers-and-local-businesses-301026271.html?mod=article_inline.

14. Kenneth P. Vogel, "The Race for Virus Money Is On. Lobbyists Are Standing By," *New York Times*, March 28, 2020, https://www.nytimes.com/2020/03/28/us /politics/coronavirus-money-lobbyists.html.

15. Michael Grunwald, phone interview by authors, April 24, 2020.

16. John Cannan, "A Legislative History of the Affordable Care Act: How Legislative Procedure Shapes Legislative History," *Law Library Journal* 105, no. 2 (2013): 131–74, https://cpb-us-w2.wpmucdn.com/sites.gsu.edu/dist/1/170/files/2014/03 /LLJ_105n2_cannan-n6ym9s.pdf.

17. Drew DeSilver, "10 Facts about American Workers," Pew Research Center, August 29, 2019, https://www.pewresearch.org/fact-tank/2019/08/29/facts-about -american-workers/.

18. Ken Sweet, "Americans Who Don't Have a Bank Account at Lowest Level Ever," AP News, October 23, 2018, https://apnews.com/8b2b93d4e9474c418853e0f2 0e79aaa8#:~:text=In%202017%20approximately%206.5%20percent,adults%20with-out%20a%20bank%20account.

19. Gabriel Zucker, Tara Dawson McGuinness, and Nina Olson, "CARES Act Stimulus Payments Have Reached 160 Million Households—but Could Reach Millions More," New America, last updated July 2, 2020, https://www.newamerica.org /public-interest-technology/reports/cares-act-stimulus-payments/.

20. Ibid.

21. "IRS to Mail Special Letter to Estimated 9 Million Non-filers, Urging Them to Claim Economic Impact Payment by Oct. 15 at IRS.gov," IRS.gov, https://www.irs .gov/newsroom/irs-to-mail-special-letter-to-estimated-9-million-non-filers-urging -them-to-claim-economic-impact-payment-by-oct-15-at-irsgov.

22. "Want to Donate Your Stimulus? Here's How Some Washingtonians Did It," NPR, April 23, 2020, https://www.npr.org/local/305/2020/04/23/842739146/want -to-donate-your-stimulus-check-here-s-how-some-washingtonians-did-it.

23. David Yaffe-Bellany, "'The Big Guys Get Bailed Out': Restaurants Vie for Relief Funds," *New York Times*, April 20, 2020, https://www.nytimes.com/2020/04/20/business/shake-shack-returning-loan-ppp-coronavirus.html.

24. Margaret Coleman, phone interview by authors, April 15, 2020.

25. IRS, "159 Million Economic Impact Payments Processed; Low-Income People and Others Who Aren't Required to File Tax Returns Can Quickly Register for Payment with IRS Non-Filers Tool," news release, June 3, 2020, https://www.irs.gov/newsroom/159-million-economic-impact-payments-processed-low-income-people-and-others-who-arent-required-to-file-tax-returns-can-quickly-register-for-payment-with-irs-non-filers-tool.

26. Silvia Amaro, "Germany Is Vastly Outspending Other Countries with Its Coronavirus Stimulus," CNBC, April 20, 2020, https://www.cnbc.com/2020/04/20/coronavirus-germany-vastly-outspends-others-in-stimulus.html.

27. Wolfgang Schmidt, phone interview by authors, May 20, 2020.

28. Ibid.

29. Derek Thompson, "Denmark's Idea Could Help the World Avoid a Great Depression," *The Atlantic*, March 21, 2020, https://www.theatlantic.com/ideas/archive/2020/03/denmark-freezing-its-economy-should-us/608533/.

30. Ruben Munsterman, "Netherlands Unveils Virus Rescue Package Worth Tens of Billions," Bloomberg, March 18, 2020, https://www.bloombergquint.com/onweb/netherlands-unveils-virus-rescue-package-worth-tens-of-billions.

31. Morrissey interview, May 7, 2020.

32. White House, Office of the Press Secretary, "Fact Sheet: Mayors Challenge to End Veteran Homelessness," June 4, 2014, https://obamawhitehouse.archives.gov/the-press-office/2014/06/04/fact-sheet-mayors-challenge-end-veteran-homelessness.

33. Morrissey interview, May 7, 2020.

34. U.S. Department of Housing and Urban Development, "Homeless Management Information Systems Budgeting and Staffing Toolkit: Resource and Cost Planning for a Sustainable HMIS Implementation," March 2011, https://files.hudexchange.info/resources/documents/HMISBudgetingStaffingTookit.pdf.

35. The data methods used to count the number of homeless are disputed. As of 2017 the White House stated that 553,742 are homeless. https://www.whitehouse.gov/wp-content/uploads/2019/09/The-State-of-Homelessness-in-America.pdf. The White House number is based on a point-in-time count that, according to field experts, does not accurately reflect the number of people experiencing homelessness. The Department of Education's (DoE) count of homeless children, which uses a different definition of homelessness, counts over a million and a half as of 2019. https://www.schoolhouseconnection.org/the-pitfalls-of-huds-point-in-time-count/.

36. Sydney Dorner, "Some Concerned about Sanitation at Springfield's Tent City," ABC, Channel 20, September 25, 2020, https://newschannel20.com/news

/local/seniors-prepare-to-fight-two-viruses-at-once. https://newschannel20.com/news/local/some-concerned-about-sanitation-at-springfields-tent-city.

37. Mike Jones, "Advocates for Homeless Mobilize as Deadline Looms," *Times Leader*, September 26, 2020, https://www.timesleaderonline.com/news/community/2020/09/advocates-for-homeless-mobilize-as-deadline-looms/.

38. Francis Fukuyama, "What's Wrong with Public Policy Education," *American Interest*, August 1, 2018, https://www.the-american-interest.com/2018/08/01/whats-wrong-with-public-policy-education/.

39. Jake Maguire, lecture to Georgetown public policy students, April 1, 2020.

40. https://www.heinz.cmu.edu/about/public-interest-technology/policy-innovation-lab.

41. Muñoz interview, April, 9 2020.

42. "Policy Basics: The Earned Income Tax Credit," Center on Budget and Policy Priorities, December 10, 2019, https://www.cbpp.org/research/federal-tax/policy-basics-the-earned-income-tax-credit#:~:text=Reducing%20Poverty,people%2C%20including%206.1%20million%20children.

43. IHI Multimedia Team, "Like Magic? ('Every System Is Perfectly Designed . . .')" *Institute for Healthcare Improvement* (blog), August 21, 2015, http://www.ihi.org/communities/blogs/origin-of-every-system-is-perfectly-designed-quote.

Chapter 5

1. "Here to There: Lessons Learned from Public Interest Law," Freedman Consulting, LLC, 2018, http://tfreedmanconsulting.com/wp-content/uploads/2019/03/Ford_Here-To-There_New-Format_20181107.pdf.

2. Matt Stempeck, "A Timeline of Civic Tech Tells a Data-Driven Story of the Field," Civic Hall, May 28, 2019, https://civichall.org/civicist/how-civic-tech-has-evolved-over-the-last-25-years/.

3. Quoted in Harlan Yu and David G. Robinson, "The New Ambiguity of 'Open Government,'" *UCLA Law Review* 59 (March 2, 2012): 186, https://papers.ssrn.com/sol3/papers.cfm?abstract_id=2012489.

4. Norman C. Thomas, "Presidential Accountability since Watergate," *Presidential Studies Quarterly* 8, no. 4 (1978): 431, www.jstor.org/stable/27547426.

5. Peter R. Orszag, "Open Government Directive," Open Government Initiative, December 8, 2009, https://obamawhitehouse.archives.gov/open/documents/open-government-directive.

6. Tim Davies, Fernando Perini, and José M. Alonso, "Researching the Emerging Impacts of Open Data: ODDC Conceptual Framework," World Wide Web Founda-

tion, July 2013, https://idl-bnc-idrc.dspacedirect.org/bitstream/handle/10625/56313/IDL-56313.pdf, p. 14.

7. Tom Steinberg, "Blimey. It Looks Like the Internets Won," mySociety, January 21, 2009, https://www.mysociety.org/2009/01/21/blimey-it-looks-like-the-internets-won/.

8. Yu and Robinson, "The New Ambiguity of 'Open Government,'" 181.

9. Teresita Perez and Reece Rushing, "The CitiStat Model: How Data-Driven Government Can Increase Efficiency and Effectiveness," Center for American Progress, April 2007, https://www.americanprogress.org/wp-content/uploads/issues/2007/04/pdf/citistat_report.pdf.

10. Sean Thornton, "Brett Goldstein Departs as Chicago's CIO/CDO," Data-Smart City Solutions, June 26, 2013, https://datasmart.ash.harvard.edu/news/article/brett-goldstein-departs-as-chicagos-cio-cdo-266.

11. News Staff, "Los Angeles Names First Chief Data Officer," Government Technology (e.Republic, August 20, 2014), https://www.govtech.com/local/LA-Names-First-Chief-Data-Officer.html.

12. "Bloomberg American Cities Initiative: 2018 American Mayors Survey," Bloomberg Philanthropies, April 2018, https://www.bbhub.io/dotorg/sites/2/2018/04/American-Mayors-Survey.pdf.

13. "Civic Analytics Network: Helping Cities Unlock the Power of Data," Harvard Kennedy School: Ash Center for Democratic Governance and Innovation, April 21, 2017, https://ash.harvard.edu/news/civic-analytics-network-helping-cities-unlock-power-data.

14. "State Chief Data Officers Network," Beeck Center, accessed June 29, 2020, https://beeckcenter.georgetown.edu/state-cdo-network/.

15. "What Works Cities," Bloomberg Philanthropies, accessed June 29, 2020, https://www.bloomberg.org/program/government-innovation/what-works-cities/#get-involved.

16. Laurel Wamsley, "Fired Florida Data Scientist Launches a Coronavirus Dashboard of Her Own," NPR, June 14, 2020, https://www.npr.org/2020/06/14/876584284/fired-florida-data-scientist-launches-a-coronavirus-dashboard-of-her-own.

17. "State CIO Top Ten Policy and Technology Priorities for 2020," NASCIO (National Association of State Chief Information Officers), December 11, 2019, https://www.nascio.org/resource-center/resources/state-cio-top-ten-policy-and-technology-priorities-for-2020/.

18. "Member Profiles," NASCIO (National Association of State Chief Information Officers), 2020, https://www.nascio.org/member-profiles/.

19. Ibid.

20. "Innovations—History," U.S. Census Bureau, accessed June 29, 2020, https://www.census.gov/history/www/innovations/.

21. David Osborne, interview by authors, December 10, 2019.

22. Stephen Goldsmith, Neil Kleiman, and Steve Case, *A New City O/S: The Power of Open, Collaborative, and Distributed Governance* (Washington, DC: Brookings Institution Press, 2017).

23. Laura Winig, *Hacking Bureaucracy: Reimagining California's Food Stamp Program in the Digital Age*, HKS Case number 2085.0, December 23, 2016 (Cambridge, MA: Harvard Kennedy School of Government, Case Program), https://case.hks.harvard.edu/hacking-bureaucracy-reimagining-californias-food-stamp-program-in-the-digital-age/.

24. Schank and Hudson, *Getting the Work Done*, 41.

25. Ibid.

26. "Office of Data and Analytics," Office of Data and Analytics, accessed June 29, 2020, https://charlottenc.gov/dataanalytics/Pages/default.aspx.

27. Laura Shunk, "How Peak Performance Is Taking Denver Employees to New Heights," Westword, November 22, 2016, https://www.westword.com/news/denver-gentrification-in-the-whittier-neighborhood-11630966.

28. Schank and Hudson, *Getting the Work Done*, 46.

29. Hana Schank and Sara Hudson, *The Government Fix* (N.p.: Sense and Respond Press, 2019).

30. "About Personal Democracy Media," accessed November 4, 2020, https://personaldemocracy.com/static-content/about-personal-democracy-media.

31. Jennifer Anastasoff and Jennifer Smith, "Mobilizing Tech Talent: Hiring Technologists to Power Better Government," September 2018, https://ourpublicservice.org/wp-content/uploads/2018/09/Mobilizing_Tech_Talent-2018.09.26.pdf.

32. Chris Allison et al., "Teaching Public Service in the Digital Age," 2020, https://www.teachingpublicservice.digital/the-course.

33. Ibid.

Chapter 6

1. William J. Baumol, *The Free-Market Innovation Machine: Analyzing the Growth Miracle of Capitalism* (Princeton, NJ: Princeton University Press, 2004).

2. Wolfgang Schmidt, Zoom interview by authors, May 20, 2020.

3. Schmidt interview, May 20, 2020.

4. James Anderson, e-mail Q&A with authors, September 29, 2020.

5. Frédéric Laloux, *Reinventing Organizations: An Illustrated Invitation to Join the Conversation on Next-Stage Organizations* (Brussels: Nelson Parker, 2016), 79.

6. Martha Lane Fox, phone interview by authors, March 5, 2020

7. Osborne interview, December 10, 2019.

8. Joe Davidson, "Mostly White Male Tech Sector Needs Government Help on Diversity," *Washington Post*, December 4, 2017, https://www.washingtonpost.com/news /powerpost/wp/2017/12/04/tech-sector-needs-uncle-sams-help-on-diversity/.

9. Emily Chang, *Brotopia: Breaking Up the Boys' Club of Silicon Valley* (New York: Portfolio, 2018), 116.

10. Graubard interview, June 26, 2020.

11. Amen Ra Mashariki, phone interview by authors, June 25, 2020.

12. Benjamin Ryan, "What 311 Calls Can Tell Us about Gentrification," The Cut, August 21, 2015, https://www.thecut.com/2015/08/what-311-calls-can-tell-us-about -gentrification.html.

13. Quoted in Deirdre Mask, *The Address Book: What Street Addresses Reveal about Identity, Race, Wealth, and Power* (New York: St. Martin's, 2020).

14. Mashariki interview, June 25, 2020.

15. Ibid.

16. Ibid.

17. Ibid.

18. Dickerson interview, June 25, 2020.

19. John Doerr, *Measure What Matters: OKRs: The Simple Idea That Drives 10x Growth* (New York: Penguin, 2017).

20. Gabe Cherry, "Built by Humans. Ruled by Computers," *Michigan Engineer*, February 5, 2019, https://news.engin.umich.edu/features/built-by-humans-ruled-by -computers/.

21. Monée Fields-White et al., "Unpacking Inequities in Unemployment Insurance," New America, September 17, 2020, https://www.newamerica.org/public -interest-technology/reports/unpacking-inequities-unemployment-insurance/.

22. Caitlin Dickerson, Seth Freed Wessler, and Miriam Jordan, "Immigrants Say They Were Pressured into Unneeded Surgeries," *New York Times*, September 29, 2020, https://www.nytimes.com/2020/09/29/us/ice-hysterectomies-surgeries-georgia .html.

23. Park interview, June 30, 2020.

Chapter 7

1. John M. Barry, *The Great Influenza: The Story of the Deadliest Pandemic in History*, rev. ed. (London: Penguin Books, 2005), 23.

2. David Osborne and Ted Gaebler, *Reinventing Government: How the Entrepreneurial Spirit Is Transforming the Public Sector* (New York: Plume, 1993), 331.

3. Schank and Hudson, *Getting the Work Done*, 27.

4. Dickerson interview, June 25, 2020.

5. The Living New Deal, "Works Progress Administration (WPA) (1935)," accessed July 9, 2020, https://livingnewdeal.org/glossary/works-progress-administration-wpa -1935/.

6. Malcolm Burnley, "How the Harvard Kennedy School Abandoned America," *Boston Magazine*, January 22, 2017, https://www.bostonmagazine.com/news/2017 /01/22/harvard-kennedy-school-america/.

7. Quoted in ibid.

8. Philip Bump, "The Percent of Employed People Working for the Federal Government Is at the Lowest Level on Record," *Washington Post*, January 9, 2015, https:// www.washingtonpost.com/news/the-fix/wp/2015/01/09/the-percent-of-employed -people-working-for-the-federal-government-is-at-the-lowest-level-on-record/.

9. Park interview, June 30, 2020.

10. Ibid.

11. Mikey Dickerson speech, SXSW Conference, March 17–22, 2015, Austin, TX.

BIBLIOGRAPHY

Álvarez, Alberto Rodríguez, Dana Chisnell, and Vivian Graubard. *User-Centered Policy: Organization Assessment.* Georgetown University, May 2020. https:// beeckcenter.georgetown.edu/wp-content/uploads/2020/05/User-Centered -Policy-Checklist_Prompts-1.pdf.

Bason, Christian. *Leading Public Design.* Chicago: Policy Press, 2017.

Bornstein, David. "A Growing Drive to Get Homelessness to Zero." *New York Times,* June 5, 2018. https://www.nytimes.com/2018/06/05/opinion/homelessness -built-for-zero.html.

Chang, Ann Mei. *Lean Impact: How to Innovate for Radically Greater Social Good.* Hoboken, NJ: John Wiley and Sons, 2018.

Chopra, Aneesh, and Ethan Skolnick. *Innovative State: How New Technologies Can Transform Government.* New York: Atlantic Monthly Press, 2014.

Chouldechova, Alexandra, Emily Putnam-Hornstein, Diana Benavides-Prado, Oleksandr Fialko, and Rhema Vaithianathan. "Conference on Fairness, Accountability, and Transparency." In *Proceedings of Machine Learning Research.* PMLR, 2018. http://proceedings.mlr.press/v81/chouldechova18a/chouldechova18a.pdf.

Cottam, Hilary. *Radical Help: How We Can Remake the Relationships between Us and Revolutionise the Welfare State.* London: Virago, 2018.

Daidone, Frank, and Benilda Samuels. "How End-User Feedback Can Become a Nonprofit's Innovation Engine." *Stanford Social Innovation Review,* January 23, 2019. https://ssir.org/articles/entry/how_end_user_feedback_can_become_a _nonprofits_innovation_engine#.

Deiglmeier, Kriss, and Amanda Greco. "Why Proven Solutions Struggle to Scale Up." *Stanford Social Innovation Review,* August 10, 2018. https://ssir.org/articles/entry /why_proven_solutions_struggle_to_scale_up.

Doerr, John. *Measure What Matters: OKRs; The Simple Idea That Drives 10x Growth.* New York: Penguin, 2017.

Eubanks, Virginia. *Automating Inequality: How High-Tech Tools Profile, Police, and Punish the Poor.* New York: St. Martin's, 2018.

Gawande, Atul. *The Checklist Manifesto: How to Get Things Right.* New York: Metropolitan Books, 2009.

Goldsmith, Stephen. "Ignore Citizens and Invite Failure." *National Civic Review* 100, no. 1 (2011): 14–18. https://www.hks.harvard.edu/publications/ignore-citizens -and-invite-failure.

Goldsmith, Stephen, Neil Kleiman, and Steve Case. *A New City O/S: The Power of Open, Collaborative, and Distributed Governance.* Washington, DC: Brookings Institution Press, 2017.

Greenway, Andrew, Ben Terrett, Mike Bracken, and Tom Loosemore. *Digital Transformation at Scale: Why the Strategy Is Delivery.* London: London Publishing Partnership, 2018.

Gregory, Alice. "R U There?" *New Yorker,* February 9, 2015. https://www.newyorker .com/magazine/2015/02/09/r-u.

Harrell, Cyd. *A Civic Technologist's Practice Guide.* N.p.: Five Seven Five Books, 2020.

Hu, Elise. "A Few Places Where Government Tech Procurement Works." NPR, November 11, 2013. https://www.npr.org/sections/alltechconsidered/2013/11/11 /243799076/a-few-places-where-government-tech-procurement-works.

Ismail, Salim, Michael S. Malone, and Yuri van Geest. *Exponential Organizations: Why New Organizations Are Ten Times Better, Faster, and Cheaper Than Yours (and What to Do about It).* New York: Diversion Books, 2014.

Karippacheril, Tina George, and Emily Tavoulareas. "Getting Digital Service Delivery Right." *World Bank Blogs* (blog), January 28, 2014. https://blogs.worldbank .org/governance/getting-digital-service-delivery-right.

Kolesar, Peter J. "What Deming Told the Japanese in 1950." In *W. Edwards Deming: Critical Evaluations in Business and Management,* edited by John C. Wood and Michael C. Wood (2005).

Loukides, Mike, Hilary Mason, and DJ Patil. *Ethics and Data Science.* Sebastopol, CA: O'Reilly Media, 2018.

Marina Martin: Innovating inside the Lines. Code for America, 2016. YouTube video. https://www.youtube.com/watch?v=GFgECfg6MzE.

McGuinness, Tara, and Anne-Marie Slaughter. "The New Practice of Public Problem Solving." *Stanford Social Innovation Review,* Spring 2019. https://ssir.org/articles /entry/the_new_practice_of_public_problem_solving.

Noveck, Beth Simone. *Smart Citizens, Smarter State: The Technologies of Expertise and the Future of Governing.* Cambridge, MA: Harvard University Press, 2015.

Osborne, David, and Ted Gaebler. *Reinventing Government: How the Entrepreneurial Spirit Is Transforming the Public Sector.* New York: Plume, 1993.

Pahlka, Jennifer. "Delivery-Driven Government: Principles and Practices for Government in the Digital Age." Medium.com, May 30, 2018. https://medium.com/code-for-america/delivery-driven-government-67e698c57c7b.

Patil, DJ, and Hilary Mason. "Data Driven: Creating a Data Culture." O'Reilly Media, December 31, 2014. https://www.oreilly.com/content/data-driven/.

Peters, Thomas J., and Robert H. Waterman. *In Search of Excellence: Lessons from America's Best-Run Companies.* Rev. ed. New York: Harper Business, 2006.

Rifkin, Jeremy. *The Zero Marginal Cost Society: The Internet of Things, the Collaborative Commons, and the Eclipse of Capitalism.* Rev. ed. New York: Griffin, 2015.

Schank, Hana, and Sara Hudson. *The Government Fix.* N.p.: Sense and Respond Press, 2019.

Thaler, Richard, and Cass Sunstein. *Nudge: Improving Decisions about Health, Wealth, and Happiness.* New Haven, CT: Yale University Press, 2008.

SUGGESTED READING
AND RESOURCES

For those wondering where to go next to learn more about public interest technology, we've put together a list of suggested reading materials, as well as organizations and networks you might want to get to know.

What to Read First

Civic Tech Field Guide, https://civictech.guide/
A Civic Technologist's Practice Guide by Cyd Harrell
Digital Transformation at Scale: Why the Strategy Is Delivery by Andrew
  Greenway, Ben Terrett, Mike Bracken, and Tom Loosemore
*Delivery-Driven Government: Principles and Practices for Government in the
  Digital Age* by Code for America, https://medium.com/code-for-america
  /delivery-driven-government-67e698c57c7b
The Government Fix by Hana Schank and Sara Hudson
*Helping Policy Makers Put People First: A Step-by-Step Tool for User Centered
  Policy Making*, https://beeckcenter.georgetown.edu/helping-policy-makers
  -put-people-first-a-step-by-step-tool-for-user-centered-policy-making/
Leading Public Design by Christian Bason
Lean Impact, https://www.annmei.com/
The US Digital Services Playbook, https://playbook.cio.gov/

Some of the Many Organizations and
Networks Building the Field
Nonprofit Organizations

Black Girls Code, https://www.blackgirlscode.com/
CityMart, https://www.citymart.com/

Civic Hall, https://civichall.org/
Code for America, https://www.codeforamerica.org/
Data 4 Black Lives, https://d4bl.org/
DataKind, https://www.datakind.org/

Benefit Delivery

Benefit Data Trust, https://bdtrust.org/
Benefit Kitchen, https://benefitkitchen.com/
mRelief, https://www.mrelief.com/
Propel, https://www.joinpropel.com/

Teaching Digital

Teaching Digital, https://www.teachingpublicservice.digital/
The Beeck Center, https://beeckcenter.georgetown.edu/
The Tech Talent Project, https://techtalentproject.org/

Fellowship Programs

Ash Center: Technology and Democracy Fellowship, https://ash.harvard.edu
    /technology-and-democracy-fellowship
Aspen Institute, https://www.aspeninstitute.org/news/press-release/tech
    -policy-hub-fellowship/
Coding It Forward, https://blog.codingitforward.com/introducing-the-2020
    -civic-digital-fellowship-8b7c8e7aafd8
Congressional Digital Service Fellowship, https://www.techcongress.io
    /congressional-digital-service
Fuse Corps, https://www.fusecorps.org/
Mozilla, https://foundation.mozilla.org/en/fellowships
Presidential Innovation Fellowship, https://presidentialinnovationfellows.gov/
Results for America Fellows, https://results4america.org/our-work/local
    -government-fellows/
TechCongress, https://www.techcongress.io/

University of Washington eScience Data Science for Social Good, https://www
.nwspk.com/fellowshipd; https://escience.washington.edu/get-involved
/incubator-programs/data-science-for-social-good/
US Digital Response [Volunteer], https://www.usdigitalresponse.org/

Networks

Alliance for Innovation, https://www.transformgov.org/
Chief Data Officers Network, https://beeckcenter.georgetown.edu
/state-cdo-network/
Civic Analytics Network, https://datasmart.ash.harvard.edu/news/article
/about-the-civic-analytics-network-826
Public Interest Technology Network, https://www.newamerica.org/public
-interest-technology/university-network/
What Works Cities, https://whatworkscities.bloomberg.org/

Newsletters Featuring Public Interest Technologists and Their Work

Apolitical, https://apolitical.co/home
The Atlas, https://the-atlas.com/
Bloomberg Spark, https://www.bloomberg.com/series/the-spark
The Commons, https://wearecommons.us/

Database of Public Interest Companies and Organizations

Civic Tech Companies and Organizations, https://airtable.com/universe
/exp8LkpapvedfTi6k/civic-tech-companies-and-organizations?explore=true

INDEX